Hideous Gnosis
Black Metal Theory Symposium 1

http://blackmetaltheory.blogspot.com

COPYRIGHT NOTICE

This work is Open Access. It is licensed under a *Creative Commons Attribution-Noncommercial-No Derivative Works Attribution 3.0 United States License*. This means that:

You are free:
- to Share — to copy, distribute and transmit the work

Under the following conditions:
- Attribution — You must attribute the work in the manner specified by the author or licensor (but not in any way that suggests that they endorse you or your use of the work).
- Noncommercial — You may not use this work for commercial purposes.
- No Derivative Works — You may not alter, transform, or build upon this work.

With the understanding that:
- Waiver — Any of the above conditions can be waived if you get permission from the copyright holder.

Other Rights — In no way are any of the following rights affected by the license:
- Your fair dealing or fair use rights;
- Apart from the remix rights granted under this license, the author's moral rights;
- Rights other persons may have either in the work itself or in how the work is used, such as publicity or privacy rights.

Notice — For any reuse or distribution, you must make clear to others the license terms of this work. The best way to do this is with a link <http://creativecommons.org/licenses/by-nc-nd/3.0/us/>.

Questions may be directed to: hideous.gnosis@gmail.com

ISBN 1450572162
EAN-13 9781450572163

Cover image by Oyku Tekten

Hideous Gnosis[†]

Black Metal Theory Symposium 1

[†] "I've seen demons / And I've been shown things that no-one should see / And I know why birds alight from cables with no-one beneath / Who's on the side of the angels / Who's on the side of Satan / God's not there anymore / I know why birds fly / No-one's there anymore" (Caïna, "Hideous Gnosis," *Mourner* [Profound Lore Records, 2007]). "He is not a return to the past; he has undergone the corruption of the 'present-day man' and nothing has more place within him than the devastation which it leaves . . . the memory of Plato, of Christianity and above all—the most hideous—the memory of modern ideas, extend behind him like fields of ashes. But between the unknown and him has been silenced the chirping of ideas, and it is through this that he is similar to 'ancient man': of the universe he is no longer the rational (alleged) master, but the dream" (Bataille, *Inner Experience*). blackmetaltheory.blogspot.com

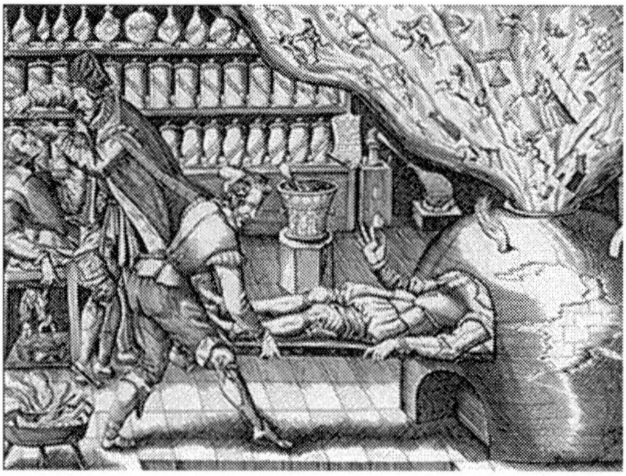

Hideous Gnosis: Black Metal Theory Symposium 1
Edited by
Nicola Masciandaro

CONTENTS

Introduction
1

Steven Shakespeare
The Light that Illuminates Itself, the Dark that Soils Itself: Blackened Notes from Schelling's Underground
5

Erik Butler
The Counter-Reformation in Stone and Metal: Spiritual Substances
23

Scott Wilson
BAsileus philosoPHOrum METaloricum
33

Hunter Hunt-Hendrix
Transcendental Black Metal
53

Nicola Masciandaro
Anti-Cosmosis: Black Mahapralaya
67

Joseph Russo
Perpetue Putesco – Perpetually I Putrefy
93

Benjamin Noys
'*Remain True to the Earth!*': Remarks on the Politics of Black Metal
105

Evan Calder Williams
The Headless Horsemen of the Apocalypse
129

Brandon Stosuy
Meaningful Leaning Mess
143

Aspasia Stephanou
Playing Wolves and Red Riding Hoods in Black Metal
157

Anthony Sciscione
'Goatsteps Behind My Steps . . .': Black Metal and Ritual Renewal
171

Eugene Thacker
Three Questions on Demonology
179

Niall Scott
Black Confessions and Absu-lution
221

DOCUMENTS

Lionel Maunz, *Pineal Eye*
233

Oyku Tekten, Symposium Photographs
239

Scott Wilson, "Pop Journalism and the Passion for Ignorance"
247

Karlynn Holland, Sin Eater I-V
251

Nicola Masciandaro and Reza Negarestani, Black Metal Commentary
257

Black Metal Theory Blog Comments
267

Letter from Andrew White
277

E.S.S.E, Murder Devour I
281 (2+8+1=11)

INTRODUCTION

A nonsovereignty, divinely impure. All that is left is to *fill the void with black*.
—Steven Shakespeare

Somewhere still farther off in the void floats the philosopher's stone, black metal.
—Erik Butler

Otherwise music is no different from the indifferent howling of the wind that black metal seeks to evoke, but always for somebody, if only just for oneself, to place oneself at the very limit of oneself where one is dissolved to NOTHING.
—Scott Wilson

Transcendental Black Metal is in fact nihilism, however it is a double nihilism and a final nihilism, a once and for all negation of the entire series of negations.
—Hunter Hunt-Hendrix

Via dissonant resonances within and among these three phenomenal nodes, black metal vibrationally unhinges the order of things, tritonely crushes all holy trinities, annihilates every binding of the chain of being.
—Nicola Masciandaro

The great luxury of the genre is, of course, the ability of the listener to unbind himself from the corpse bride.
—Joseph Russo

The permanence of conflict attests to the ever-receding utopian hope of the abolishing of the present, whilst also preserving a consistent and stabilised enmity to that present that gives the supplement of identity and integration – the affirmation of Black Metal as the centre of the whirlwind.
—Benjamin Noys

Despite the constant lip service to the affective portrait of the loner individual, we should venture the contrary: *black metal has no individuals, and it has no leaders.*
—Evan Calder Williams

Black metal is the fiery combustion of a romantic ideal. I think the Europeans succeeded in becoming characters larger than themselves, and that's one of my worst fears: That I will somehow create a character that lives my own life without me.
—He Who Crushes Teeth

Wolves scream in thrilled terror or mournful tones, calling forth their evil father.
—Aspasia Stephanou

He withdraws into a liminal space that exceeds the capacity for mortality to withstand it, and undergoes a sacrificial demise in order to open himself up as a habitat for and an expression of the power of the demon.

—Anthony Sciscione

A philosophical demonology would therefore have to be "against" the human being – both the "human" part as well as the "being" part.

—Eugene Thacker

Instead of the power of prohibition and censorship Black Metal Theory serves to increase and expand more and more on that which has been forbidden.

—Niall Scott

HIDEOUS GNOSIS

THE LIGHT THAT ILLUMINATES ITSELF, THE DARK THAT SOILS ITSELF: BLACKENED NOTES FROM SCHELLING'S UNDERGROUND
Steven Shakespeare

Goodbye Orlando: Black Metal and Nature

*I will lay down my bones among the rocks and roots of the deepest
  hollow next to the streambed
The quiet hum of the earth's dreaming is my new song
When I awake, the world will be born anew*
   (Wolves in the Throne Room, 'I Will Lay Down
   My Bones Among the Rocks and Roots')

'Nature is fucking crazy. No really, it is. Hippies and Greenpeace types attempt to paint it as some serene, peaceful thing filled with sunny days and baby seals, but spend an afternoon watching National Geographic documentaries and you'll see: Mother Nature can be one bloody, brutal bitch . . . Although black metal's roots are anchored in the dark, icy wastes of Scandinavia, the genre's devotion to evil, borderline clownish stage attire has lead it away from its initial, sunless inspiration. Grown men in makeup taking Satan way too seriously turned metal into a cartoonish parody of itself and left its ideology feeling hollow. After all, doesn't belief in the devil imply faith in the Christian theology? And really, just how "evil" is penning songs about corpse-fucking while you live in an Orlando apartment complex? . . . Much like the Puritans of colonial America, Wolves [in the Throne Room] discard the pompous pageantry of its European brothers to stake out an austere existence in the unsettled wilderness.'[1]

'Hippies? You mean like navel-gazing aficionados of the grateful dead [sic]? I hardly think so. I think that most people are so disconnected from a natural existence that anyone who doesn't see the joy in playing "first person shooters" or dining regularly at pizza hut is a hippie . . .

To us, the driving impulse of BM is more about deep ecology than anything else and can best be understood through the application of eco-psychology. Why are we sad and miserable? Because our modern culture has failed—we are all failures. The world around us has failed to sustain our humanity, our spirituality. The deep woe inside black metal is about fear—that we can never return to the mythic, pastoral world that we crave on a deep subconscious level. Black Metal is also about self loathing, for modernity has transformed us, our minds, bodies and spirit, into an alien life form; one not suited to life on earth without the mediating forces of technology, culture and organized religion. We are weak and pitiful in our strength over the earth—in conquering, we have destroyed ourselves. Black Metal expresses disgust with humanity and revels in the misery that one finds when the falseness of our lives is revealed.

---

[1] Devon Tincknell, 'Wolves In The Throne Room at Emo's,' <http://www.avclub.com/austin/articles/wolves-in-the-throne-room-at-emos,28924/>.

Our music, then, is not "true" Black Metal for we have moved beyond this fantasy of a nihilistic apocalypse; beyond our own misery and failure. Our music is balanced in that we temper the blind rage of Black Metal with the transcendent truths of the universe that reveal themselves with age and experience. Our relationship with the natural world is a healing force in our lives.'[2]

Black metal and nature: a betrayal of roots, or a new baptism of the earth? In any case, can this relationship be thought apart from the 'truth', the authenticity of a fantasy of origins? Is the embrace of nature particularly associated with black metal-related bands and projects of Cascadia—Wolves in the Throne Room, Fauna, Blood of the Black Owl, Echtra, Alda, Skagos, Chasma, Leech, Threnos and many others—a 'hippy' romanticism, a far right celebration of blood and soil, an American primordialist vision of the virgin wilderness/brutal mother? Or can it also offer an aural thinking of nature that troubles such 'truths'?

Mouths Filled with Soil: *Rain* by Fauna

> *You are a daughter of heaven*
> *12 stars circle your brow*
> *But you do not see them and the rain pours down*
> *Our time in this garden is past*
>   (Wolves in the Throne Room, '(A Shimmering Radiance) Diadem of 12 Stars')

---

[2] Bradley Smith, 'Interview with Wolves in the Throne Room 2006,' <http://www.nocturnalcult.com/WITTRint.htm>.

For five minutes, silence. No—not silence. There is something: is it the hiss of tape, an accidental ambience? Then, without any change, it resolves itself: the sound is gently falling rain. Persistent, saturating, gravity made visible.

And then the rain is suppressed. A different sound begins: the strumming and arpeggios of an acoustic guitar. It takes its time, building in speed. Eventually a grating, drawn out vocal emerges, stripped raw.

Before the stars fled our sky
When we spoke the old tongue
When our mouths were filled with soil
Our tongues danced like trees

The lyric mouths its own inability to speak a clear word. The old tongue chokes on the earth that feeds it.

The architecture of the song is a series of leaps. Each section seems as if it could go on for ever, repetitive, trance-like. The transitions are violent. After twenty minutes, there is an explosion of noise, as if being has broken loose of its tranquillity.

Shadow unto shadow falls
The wrung earth stills
Smoke rises from an empty face
Inkstain from the heart spreads

Hot tears spill from the sky's open seam
An ash breeze pours from our pure mouths

There is a multiplication of shadows and the earth writhes. There is no rest in this nature, no Eden. Spirit is here, but it is a tainted breath. The word rises like smoke, ink stains like blood, tears falling from a wounded heaven like semen. The purity which is envisaged by the song is not that of transparency to truth, to spirit, to the face of the other. This face is empty. The song is an ash breeze, a spiritual toxicity, an unclean emission.

The ferocity and speed ebb and flow from black thrash to doom and back. Like an animal caught in a snare. Like a vortex.

As animals we gather
Around the womb-hole in the ground
Shed this flimsy skin
Unite our eyes again

Shadow opens
Nature's hands unfold

Nature punctures skin, it is an opening, a folding of shadow. Becoming animal, we look for birth beyond the human.

Burrow deep in blackest earth
And break further

Nature breaks us. Its blackness, the blackness of earth, corrodes the solidity of existence from within. I emerge, *Hands blackened with my own blood*, myself the gutted beast whose *abyssal chest is filled with leaves*. I have become the open seam, the wound that cannot be filled, where the heart was, where the 'I' reigned, there is a void.

I great wound, the wind whips
Disappear

Feedback, echoing vibration lead the song into nothing. The ugly past curls into the fire and there are only shadows which cast their figures into the swallowing mist. Nothing of substance. A black residue of ash. An echo.

The Music of the Absolute

What does the absolute sound like? If being is known only in becoming, is the music of the spheres known only as they shatter, and grate, and scourge space and time into new forms of chaos?

Music has of course been a preoccupation of philosophers in search of harmony, of the inarticulate order of things. Resonance: the sound of a world that belongs together. According to Hegel, music is 'spirit, soul which resounds immediately for itself and feels satisfied in hearing itself [*in ihrem Sichvernehmen*].'[3]

Of course, music can't hold all the answers, not least because it cannot speak. For Hegel, instrumental music was art on a lower level. It lacked the concrete expression of the idea. There had to

---

[3] Hegel, *Aesthetics. Lectures on Fine Art*, trans. T.M. Knox, 2 vols. (Oxford: Clarendon Press, 1975), 2: 939, translation altered by Stephen Houlgate at <http://plato.stanford.edu/entries/hegel-aesthetics/>.

be words, if spirit was truly to recognise itself and hear itself. So in a sense, if music is absolute, it is dissolute: a betrayal of spirit. A blockage in spirit's ears, soil in spirit's mouth.

Kierkegaard gives perhaps the best undermining commentary on Hegel's theory of music. Kierkegaard's indirect communication, his redoubling of the absolute, is deployed to best effect in his satires on the Hegelian dialectic. That dialectic wants to return home to itself, but Kierkegaard multiplies the abysses which forever separate spirit from its own proper form. In *The Sickness Unto Death*, for example, the Hegelian analysis of the self in relation to its other in the opening pages is subverted by a constant exposure of the wounded nature of selfhood, a self established by an other power not in its grasp. The parody of redoubling commentary blisters the spirit's skin.

This wound is held open in another singular way in *Either/Or*. In the essay 'The Immediate Erotic Stages or the Musical Erotic', supposedly written by an anonymous aesthete, Mozart's *Don Giovanni* is hailed as the epitome of the musical classic. In many ways, the analysis echoes that of Hegel. But echoes are never pure, they always trace the path of a distortion.

The essay argues that music is the expression of sensuous immediacy, but it is an expression which is qualified by its relation to spirit and the idea. So far, so Hegelian—as is the focus on opera as the ultimate musical art form, where sound and text go together. Music, it seems, is only valid when watched over by the word.

However, there the echo begins to fall to ground. For Don Giovanni does not lead us to the reconciliation of the sensuous and the spiritual. It is a work of exuberant, uncaring, affirmation of the sensual and the seductive. The spirit appears only to judge the seducer, to drag Don Giovanni unrepentant into hell. But far from dispelling the sensuous, this only redoubles its intensity. The sensuous is not simply natural desire, but desire named and excluded by spirit, specifically by Christianity. In the process, the sensuous borrows something of the nature of spirit, of its conscious immortality. Spirit is infected, the echo distorts.

Here is what this invented author says about the nature of music:

'sensuousness in its elemental originality is the absolute theme of music. The sensuous in its essential nature is absolutely lyrical, and in music it erupts with all its lyrical impatience. That is, it is qualified by spirit and therefore is power, life movement, continual unrest, continual succession. But this unrest, this succession, does not enrich it; it continually remains the same; it does not unfold but incessantly rushes forward as if in a single breath. If I were to describe this lyricism with a single predicate, I would have to say—It sounds [*den toner*].'[4]

It reverberates, it rings out. Power, life, movement, a restless, unyielding spirit, never at home, at one. It rushes forward. It sounds and re-sounds without atonement.

Does music then lead us to worship vitality and life itself? Is music nature as opposed to spirit? Hardly, if what we mean by

---

[4] Kierkegaard, *Either/Or Part One* (Princeton: Princeton University Press, 1988), p. 71.

as it ceases to be the serving centrum and enters as ruling into the periphery, it burns in I-hood as the selfish and egotistical rage (of enflamed I-hood) of Tantalus . . . in one single place of the planetary system this dark centrum of nature is closed up, latent, and for that very reason serves as a carrier of light for the entry of the higher system (illumination or revelation of the ideal). For that very reason this place is thus the open point (sun-heart-eye) in the system and, if the dark centrum of nature were also to raise or open itself there, then the light point would *eo ipso* close itself up, light would become darkness in the system or the sun would be extinguished!' (Franz Baader, quoted EF 35n)

Into the periphery . . . enflamed rage . . . a burning centre. The eye blinded, the sun made dark. A subversion: the dark periphery of nature surging up into the open place of the light. Until we cannot decide where the centre lies, and where it *lies*.

Nature becomes: nature is the becoming of being, and black metal allows us to hear its subterranean roar. On the album *A Feral Spirit*, Ruhr Hunter/Blood of the Black Owl's ritualistic black metal initiates us into multiple becomings: with and into nature. But this is nature without reconciliation.

We are born of the elk . . .
Yet on the outside of her body
Our skin burns on the cold ground

We are the earth . . .
And again we go back to the earth . . .
And our skin burns on the cold ground

Becoming animal, but excluded from essence . . . skin no longer remains a carrier of light. The human subject is dethroned, but no natural immediacy takes its place.

I was the atavism
At eve I would leave my fortress
The endless dirt of the road
Becoming my skin

Are we disembodied? Never finally. The skin is a passage, a mutation.

Blood to blend with soil and rock
Transcendental hallucinatory river
I become these climbs

The music howls and groans, Sabbath slow. Descending chords lead us back to the portal of the forest . . . my soul will sink away *becoming the trees, the moss, this forest of miasmic decrepitude.* There are *unseen horrors*, twisting and turning . . . *all of this is mine.* A pastoral interlude is briefly forgotten. It offers nature's mourning. Suffocation returns—mouths choked by soil, speaking an ash breeze. It sounds . . .

The trees no longer speak, to us...
The birds have ceased to sing...
We wear the skins...
Of the carrion fowl...
We cannibalize our dead...
Our faces are worn...
With the gallows mask...
The soil is tilled...

With bones...

No whispers of naïve old legends in the forest. No building up of some secure identity: *The soul never existed—neither did you...* These woods/words are an ecstatic decay . . .

My personal mausoleum
Sprawling Woodlands
Of no life
My beloved putrescent kingdom

The sun is extinguished. A darkness at noon over the scourged body become dirt, become curse. A nonsovereignty, divinely impure. All that is left is to *fill the void with black*.

Profaning the Ground

For Schelling, behind God lies a primordial ground, an unconditioned absolute. From this ground, an unconscious will arises. It is a will to know itself as absolute. The unconditioned is 'the will that wills nothing (AW 132). 'It is the pure freedom itself that does not grasp itself, it is the composure [*Gelassenheit*] that thinks about nothing and rejoices in its nonbeing' (AW 134). From the abyss, the *Abgrund*, being and existence coalesce. The will seeks to express itself in reality, in the manifold, in 'what-is'—but being acts as the magnetic force which draws all things back to its black heart. 'A counterstriving imposes itself everywhere; everyone feels this other force, which, as it were, should not be, but nevertheless is – indeed, it must be. [It is] this No that opposes the Yes, this darkness that opposes the light, this crooked that opposes the straight, this left that opposes the right' (AW 140).

Schelling identifies the expansive force of existence with love, which implies an identification of being with hate. Certainly, it can be expressed as the jealous intolerance of difference, the will to dissolve all things back into the ground. It is the wrath of God. But without it, love would be a vanishing mist, a groundless, natureless lack. Light and dark are not just necessary contrasts. The one inhabits the other as its inner, parasitic, constitutive core. As Zizek says of the ground, 'God needs this foreign body in his heart' (AW 6), even though it corrodes his identity and existence from within.

The possibility of evil arises from the ground no longer keeping its place. When the ground rises up and wants to rule, the proper order of things is knocked awry. But in a sense, the proper order has always already been out of joint. God cannot simply suppress or annihilate the ground: '. . . God does not now resist the will of the ground or abolish it. This would be precisely as much as to say that God would abolish the condition of his existence, that is, his own personality. Thus, in order that there be no evil, there would have to be no God himself' (EF 65-66).

When ground is elevated over existence 'a life emerges which, though individual, is, however, false, a life of mendacity, a growth of restlessness and decay' (EF 34). But this is not an accidental restlessness and decay. It is a lie lodged in the dissonance of spirit itself. As individual spiritual beings, we need to step out of the black hole of the ground in order not to be consumed, but this necessary dislocation is also the possibility of evil: 'All life first becomes and develops in the night' (AW 179).

Schelling remains an idealist, not only philosophically but in the broadest sense of the term. He wants to see the ground kept in place, reduced to mere potency by the freedom of light and spirit. But as he says, 'Idealism, if it does not have as its basis a living realism, becomes just as empty and abstract a system as that of Leibniz, Spinoza, or any other dogmatist.' (EF 26)—and few have attempted as he has to hold the speculative absolute entwined with the corrosive and constitutive power of being and nature. When Schelling writes of 'the reversed god' which seeks 'by means of mirrorlike images to bring man to the senselessness in which it alone can be understood and accepted by him' (EF 54-55), the reversal of which he speaks is a Satanic abyss that was always within God.

If there is a recovery of nature in Schelling's philosophy—against those philosophies which vaunt subjectivity and reason over against nature—it is not a return to any lost Eden: 'the true stuff of all life and existence is the horrible' (AW 17, quoted by Zizek). Sin fills us with horror because it 'strives to break the word, touch the ground of creation, and profane the mystery' (EF 55). But this 'sin', this profanity, this self-touching of the ground is not the opposite of light and spirit. It is the friction, the irritation, without which light is dissipated and spirit does not amount even to a shadow.

The buzzsaw guitar, the all too audible crudity of the production process: an aural friction, a scoured glass of sound. Do these enable us to hear nature differently, breaking the spell of reflection which seeks to bind everything in its proper place?

You watch me face the mirror
And see desecration
With my art I am the fist
In the face of God.
    (Darkthrone, 'To Walk the Infernal Fields')

A simple rage? A simple opposition? Or does another dissonance emerge? What if this art, this breaking of the image, this fist in the face God, what if this were the condition for revelation? Revelation would therefore also be a matter of desecration, and vice versa. Revelation, not of purity, but of the always soiled absolute, the always crucified God.

THE COUNTER-REFORMATION IN STONE AND METAL: SPIRITUAL SUBSTANCES
Erik Butler

This paper places the late-twentieth- and early-twenty-first-century phenomenon of "black metal" in an early modern context, which in turn evokes still earlier times: the Middle Ages of Europe, Christian and otherwise. Black metal, although a musical youth culture, can be better understood in relation to the history of religion. Insofar as it operates by analogy, the mode of argument here is open to critique. However, because the claims presented develop the implications of the way black-metal practitioners define their craft, they are not arbitrary or overly speculative. The following remarks respect the internal categories of black metal; my commentary merely draws out the implications of others' discourse. Admittedly, there is some irony in analyzing a northern, pagan cultural movement in this way. However, the paradoxes inhere in black metal itself.

I. The Early Modern Church

The sixteenth-century Council of Trent sought, in the face of Renaissance humanism and Protestant Reformation, to strengthen the institutional columns of the church erected in medieval times: notably–besides church doctrine–the importance of works and sacraments for salvation. Pilgrimages, relics, and the cult of Mary affirmed the centrality of embodied practice in this world as a portal to the next.[1]

Among monastic orders, the Society of Jesus (or Jesuits, as they came to be known) took the lead in propagating the faith and the practices that underpinned it.[2] Fittingly, their motto *Ad maiorem Dei gloriam*, "for the greater glory of God," has been appropriated and modified by the black metal group Gorgoroth, who have entitled a release *Ad Majorem Sathanas Gloriam*.[3] The slogan wrested from the *ecclesia militans*, or "church militant," points toward the rhetorical, aesthetic, and ideological aims of black metal.

Before turning to proselytizing Satanists, however, other aspects of Jesuitical rigor and Counter-Reformation belief and practice warrant mention. The Society of Jesus is known for its intellectualism, cultural pursuits, and social activism. Time does not permit a lengthy discussion of the latter two points—the Jesuits' educational missions and activities in Asia and South America were deemed politically subversive and led to a suspension of the order from 1773 to 1814—but they are important to bear in mind, as they display morphological

---

[1] For a presentation and reevaluation of the facts upon which scholars have come to agree—including the phrase "Counter Reformation"—see John Bireley, *The Refashioning of Catholicism, 1450-1700: A Reassessment of the Counter Reformation* (Washington, DC: Catholic University of America Press, 1999).

[2] An overview of the attitudes in question is found in the short book by William A. Barry, S.J., and Robert G. Doherty, S.J., *Contemplatives in Action: The Jesuit Way* (Mahwah, N.J.: Paulist Press, 2002); Jonathan Wright, *God's Soldiers: Adventure, Politics, Intrigue, and Power—A History of the Jesuits* (Garden City, NY: Image, 2005) offers a history along the lines the book's title indicates.

[3] Regain Records, 2006.

similarity to aspects of the black metal phenomenon, which likewise seeks to disseminate "teachings" of is own and often is affiliated with radical politics (albeit of a right-wing variety).

Roland Barthes has drawn attention to the "obsessional character" of the *Spiritual Exercises*, the guide to devotion written by the founder of the order, Saint Ignatius of Loyola (1491[?]-1556). At the same time, and somewhat paradoxically, Jesuitical spirituality and practice are distinguished by the ambition of *indifference* to the deceptions of the sublunary world. The point on which these conflicting aims hinge is a revaluation of the senses, which, while adhering to the Judeo-Christian primacy of hearing, makes new room for the power of sight. Barthes writes:

> to . . . mistrustings of the image Ignatius responded with a radical imperialism of the image: [a] product of the guided imagination, the image is the abiding material of the *Exercises*. . . . [T]he sights, representations, allegories, [and] mysteries . . . constantly created by the image-making senses are the constitutive units of meditation.[4]

The *Exercises* fight fire with fire, as it were. Instead of fleeing the world of illusion, Jesuits counter it with their own discipline of image-creation. This attitude of steeling oneself against the storm of fallible, fleshly impressions keeps the soldier of God on the right path. He conducts himself according to a mortifying code that guards against error. In the language of the Society of Jesus, the Christian soldier is *perinde ac cadaver*: "like a corpse."[5]

---

[4] Roland Barthes, *Sade, Fourier, Loyola*, trans. Richard Miller (Berkeley: University of California Press, 1989), 66.

[5] Barthes, 73.

II. The "Protestant Heresy"

What is the Protestant heresy in music? There are numerous indictments to be made, but the principal perversions of devotional forms, in the eyes of the self-appointed heavy metal "elite," would have to include disco and punk. Although the differences between these two types of music are readily apparent, disco and punk originate and evolve at the same historical moment and reject inherited practices and sacrosanct tradition.

Disco combines black, urban, and gay cultures.[6] In addition, it augments rock instrumentation with heavily percussive elements, of Latin American and Caribbean provenance, as well as orchestral arrangements (notably brass and strings). The disco sound relies on lengthy musical periods and induces a trancelike state in listeners, who are called upon to commune in dance. Its spirit is ecstatic and revivalist—a kind of "baptism" in music.

Punk, in contrast, is noisy, abrasive, and stripped-down. Technical ability is deemphasized, hence the famous call for anyone who can play three chords to start a band of their own. Punk also refuses the cheerful (or, alternately, sentimental) attitude of disco. However, punk evinces similarities with its unlikely counterpart inasmuch as its protest—which, if you will, is Calvinist and iconoclastic—breaks dramatically with the inheritance of the preceding musical age. "Never trust a hippie," goes a slogan popular in the punk community.

---

[6] See Peter Shapiro, *Turn the Beat Around: The Rise and Fall of Disco* (New York: Faber & Faber, 2007).

In contrast—and somewhat improbably—heavy metal continues the legacy of the 1960s. Scholars and fans agree that the musical style was forged by Black Sabbath, a group founded in 1968. Black Sabbath's music, both formally and thematically, reacted to contemporary "flower power" while retaining key elements. The band continued the pro-drug, anti-war, psychedelic style but turned received attitudes and musical idioms in a different direction (notably through lyrical content and the prominent use of the tritone interval). The result was a sound that was darker and starker, as was the correlative vision. Whereas hippies indulged in archaizing evocations of Arcadia, Black Sabbath preferred to focus on the troubles besetting mankind since the Fall, which persist in the modern age.

III. Black Metal as Symbolism: *Fleurs du mal*

Black metal, whose shriek of birth occurred in the 1980s and achieved full articulation in the early 1990s, represents a return to orthodoxy after an interlude of laxness. The enemy was not only to be found outside of the metal community, but also within. The bane of so-called "hair metal," which vulgarized the art and sought commercial success is the most egregious example.[7] Closer to the citadels of black, monastic piety there was also the threat of "death metal."[8] While formally and

---

[7] Ian Christe, *Sound of the Beast: The Complete Headbanging History of Heavy Metal* (New York: HarperCollins, 2003), 153-71.

[8] The genesis of this style and connections to the related genre of "grindcore" are chronicled by Albert Mudrian, *Choosing Death: The Improbable History of Death Metal and Grindcore* (Los Angeles: Feral House, 2004).

genetically connected with black metal in many ways (via thrash metal), and also a response to over-commodification, death metal is fundamentally a different beast. Celebrating blood, gore, and bodily functions, it has a worldly orientation, or at any rate exists in a continuum with impermanent matter, monstrous growth and decay. Reference to Satan, when it is made, seeks only to affirm the sinful flesh.

One of the most striking features of black metal as a consolidated entity (that is, in the 1990s), is the stress placed on "purity," a spiritual—indeed, a Gnostic—emphasis that distinguishes it from competing forms of heavy metal and all but its most "ancient" predecessor, Black Sabbath. Black metal emphasizes the Rock of Ages, as it were, the Satanic Cult Eternal. The lexicon of black metal is comprised, to an extent unmet by other forms of music, of references to the enduring, the abiding, and the transcendent: the arctic tundra, the unyielding night of the northern winter, virgin woods and wastelands, stone, mountains, the moon, and the stars. "Hordes," as the groups are often called, employ logos that are meant to be read only with utmost difficulty, like magical sigils. Album art is almost always devoid of colors other than the fundamental binary black/white. Finally, performers mask themselves in "corpse paint," *perinde ac cadaver*. While the faculty of hearing of course remains paramount—this is music, after all— an Ignatian "imperialism of images" frames the experience and is woven into its very fabric.

IV. Exemplum: *Pure Holocaust* by Immortal

A fuller vitality beyond mere life and death is the object of Immortal's cult. The Norwegian necromancers use sound and fury to cross the boundaries separating the world here from the greater world beyond. The metal *sub specie aeternitatis* of Immortal pierces the veil of appearances to summon, in the words of Goethe, "the spirit that negates."[9] The album begins:

Spiritless I Lay On Cryptic Stones
Mesmerising Snow Wait Silent Above Me
And My Yearn For Frost Grow Strongly.
I Am Demon
[. . .]
Awaiting To See The Dawnless Realms . . . .[10]

The scene is one of incubation, a summoning of otherworldly forces to take possession of the sleeper. The spirit is not in the flesh, but must arrive from elsewhere. This immersion in darkness suspends the rules that govern waking life, and it rests upon the fundament of another law: the cosmic cycle of seasons, itself a part of the course of astral bodies. The cold wind blows from beyond the Earth's atmosphere—descending from on high. And lo!, the visionary declares "I Am Demon"—existing between action and rest, life and death, self and other. The state reproduces the symbolist experience described by Arthur Rimbaud, author of the "Alchimie du verbe" (*Une saison en enfer*): "JE est un autre."[11]

---

[9] Johann Wolfgang von Goethe, *Goethe's Faust*, trans. Walter Kaufmann (New York: Anchor Books, 1962), 161.

[10] Lyrics are taken from the booklet accompanying *Pure Holocaust* (Osmose Productions, 1993).

[11] Arthur Rimbaud, *Complete Works and Selected Letters*, trans. Wallace Fowlie (Chicago: University of Chicago Press, 1966), 304.

Time permitting, the connection to nineteenth-century poetry and what Mario Praz called "the Romantic agony" might be explored further. One more passage from *Pure Holocaust* will have to suffice. Canto III:

In The Mist of Twilight
You Could See Me Come
[. . .]
Sempiternal Woods Wait Only for Me
A Path Opens Clearly
The Sun No Longer Rises

This hymn, for the first time in the lyrical journey, addresses a second person. The advent of the horde-I, the expansive voice that has grown ever louder since announcing "I Am Demon" takes place "In The Mist Of Twilight," that is, at a threshold moment in time, which in turn corresponds to the threshold experience of the swarming warrior band, a single yet multiple entity. Like the sudden precipitation of solid matter in a murky solution, the clouds part and "A Path Opens Clearly." The path is clear because its unambiguous blackness parts the gaseous, gray nebulas of earthly illusion.

The heaviest metal found on Earth is uranium; enriched uranium is plutonium, a substance that conjures up the Lord of the Dead. Heavier elements occur only in space, where Pluto mournfully orbits the Sun at a distance of 3,666 million miles. Somewhere still farther off in the void floats the philosopher's stone, black metal. If the Thessalian witches described by the Mediterranean poets Ovid and Lucan pulled down the moon with their obscure arts, their Norwegian counterparts Immortal pass beyond the Moon, Jupiter, Saturn, Mars, Neptune, and even Pluto—that is, they gallop beyond the horizon of classical antiquity and modern science alike—to where "The Sun No Longer Rises" and "The Eternity Opens" (Canto VII). *Pure Holocaust* is Immortal's cosmic aim: the harnessing of black metal, the beginning and end of the dark universe in which our piteous globe hangs suspended.

BAsileus philosoPHOrum METaloricum
Scott Wilson

> Seeking death . . . I ride the longing winds of my blackened soul eternally.
> Emperor, 'Ye Entrancemperium' (1997)

> It is in death that black metal finds its infinite resourcefulness; the approach of death—its sovereign gesture, its prominence within human memory—hollows out in the present and in existence the void toward which and from which black metal resounds.
> Michel Foucault (1986, 53)[1]

1. The Blackened Symposium

Already, with the notion of a symposium, there is the expectation that music and speech will conjoin and, moreover, conjoin 'with drinking' (*sum-posion*). Most famously of all, Plato's *Symposium* records a somewhat drunken dialogue on love and beauty from the 4th Century BC. Given the misanthropy that characterizes black metal, we might suppose that the Black Metal Theory Symposium will be more concerned with hatred, but one does not come without the other. For the love of black metal we side with 'the great adversary' of existence (Nortt, in Stosuy, 2008). It is indeed a question of love and hatred and precisely not of judgement, for there is no possibility of conjunction between black metal and academic discourse in any other way since the whole point of critical judgement is to take the former for its object and place it under the spotlight,

---

[1] Some quotations drawn from noted theorists have been 'blackened' in an obvious and playful way in order to highlight affinities between theory and black metal.

illuminate the darkness, set up a beacon in the obscure heart of the forest and flash an investigative torch into its sallow face.

Black metal and academic discourse are no doubt heterogeneous and cannot be conjoined, but in bringing one into proximity with the other it is essential that this clash should result less in the academic illumination of black metal than in the blackening of discourse itself wherein the forces of black metal restore some of the powers and dangers of discourse which the procedures of academic institutions seek to ward off and master by controlling and delimiting them. There is a long history of such procedures but currently they are more often than not justified with reference to 'ethical' judgements concerning representations and the 'power relations' they are supposed to reproduce and re-instantiate, judgements that do nothing other than draw a work into the University's own nexus of power/knowledge by which, as a biopolitical function of the state, it seeks to manage and regulate it in the name of health, life and utility.

Black metal can bring its forces to discourse by drawing it into the freezing orbit of its sonic density so that, suspended between life and the death that opens it to infinity, academic speech might become drawn out of itself, erase itself for the exclusive sovereignty of that which it wishes to say and which lies outside of words. Heterogeneous to language, music, of course, refers to nothing but itself in the universe of sound except, perhaps, voice. Speech enters into the music and becomes it (becomes song) even as it dies, disappearing *as* music, breathing its last endless rasping breath, the great breath that simulates a theory of breathing linked by so many threads to the whole of Western philosophy, and yet which emerges from it, rendering permeable the limits of discourse.

This piece will suggest and perform various ways in which black metal permeates and 'blackens' academic discourse across four polarities: the subject, knowledge, non-knowledge and truth. In so doing it must displace academic conventions so that there is a constant contamination of force and affinity between black metal and discourse rather than the hierarchy of primary text and the commentary which decodes, recodes and re-states it interminably. Only in this way might commentary hope to have some bearing on 'the art to come' (Deleuze, 1995, 135). By way of example, I here invoke (as I have been throughout) Michel Foucault, that great adversary of commentary, whose theories of power have been catastrophically deployed by the institutions of liberal governance to the very purposes they were designed to undermine.

At the very end of his life, in the guise of a masked philosopher, Foucault dreamt 'about a kind of criticism that would not try to judge. . . it would light fires, like a blaze in the Northern sky, catch the sea-foam in the breeze and scatter it. It would multiply, not judgements, but signs of existence in the freezing fog, make diabolic shapes float by out from the dark; it would summon them, drag them from their sleep. Perhaps it would invent them sometimes—all the better. All the better. . . . I'd like a criticism of scintillating leaps of the imagination [that] would bear the lightning of possible storms' (Foucault, 1988, 326). This lightning, that gives 'a dense and black intensity to the night it denies', conjures an enlightenment that is at the same time a chaotic storm, 'which lights up the night from the inside, from top to bottom, and yet owes to the dark the stark clarity of its manifestation, its harrowing and poised singularity: the flash loses itself in this space it marks with its sovereignty and becomes silent now that it has given a name to obscurity' (Foucault, 1986, 34).

But as the light goes out and the voices are stilled, the wind yet whispers beside the deep forest that gives its name to this obscurity in which 'Darkness will show us the way . . .' (Mayhem, 'De Mysteriis Dom Sathanas', 1994).

2. Basileus

> Bataille's concept of sovereignty corresponds to the noncontractual liberty which is congenital with the warrior function.
>
> Denis Hollier (1988, 39)

> When you play black metal you don't play it like you were a human . . . no no no, you play it like you're a warrior.
>
> Raffi (in Kahn-Harris, 2007, 38).

> You play it like a warrior.
>
> Legion, Marduk (in Kahn-Harris, 2007, 40).

Mayhem, Emperor, Darkthrone, Beherit, Gorgoroth . . . the names of some of black metal's most exalted bands would seem to bring together the sovereign anomie that Giorgio Agamben suggests characterizes the current state of affairs, 'the state of exception' that is turning Western democracies into totalitarian states (Agamben, 2005). But this is exactly what needs to be refused, just as certainly as the temptation to assign to black metal the status of symptom: the exceptional symptom of the exception in which the fascism immanent to Western democracy enjoys itself in its pure negativity. Agamben cites Pseudo-Archytas's treaty *On Law and Justice*, in which the word

Basileus is translated as 'sovereign' rather than 'king' because it 'lays the foundations for a conception of sovereignty that is entirely unbound by laws and yet is itself the source of legitimacy' (Agamben, 2005, 70). This distinction is essential, but not for the reason Agamben finds in Pseudo-Archytas where 'the distinction between the sovereign (*basileus*), who is the law, and the magistrate (*arkhōn*), who must only observe the law, is made the origin of twentieth-century *Führerprinzip* and of Carl Schmitt's theories on dictatorship. In the space opened by the severance of law and violence, a severance that implies a doubling of violence, Agamben fantasises about 'a word that does not bind, that neither commands nor prohibits anything, but says only itself', a word that would name an utopian state of unfettered 'use and human praxis that the powers of law and myth had sought to capture in the state of exception' (88). But there is no word that does not bind or prohibit or kill that which it names. Except, perhaps, the name of a loving God . . .

Satanic laughter erupts from deep in the forest. Agamben has no place there, even if the distinction first made by Pseudo-Archytas must remain: *basileus* should be translated as sovereign rather than king and legislator. *Basileus* is that name that names only itself thereby sacrificing itself, giving way to the sovereign force of music (*a*music) that can be felt only in warrior-like play. The warrior is a conceptual character that figures that 'aspect that is opposed to the servile and the subordinate', an aspect to which a beggar might be as close as any nobleman' (Bataille, 1991, 197). So just as Agamben has no place there, neither does sociological discourse that can say nothing about the metaphor of the warrior even as it reduces art to social behaviour in its imperative to conjure-up ever more monstrous instances of paternal authority in fantasies of mastery and control that have no other purpose than to justify its own disciplinarity.

'When you play black metal you don't play it like you were a human . . . you play it like you're a warrior'. The warrior is a metaphor, a character, you can't BE a warrior, the warrior is not human, nor is s/he in-human either, but completely other to the slavish being that takes itself for a form and a universal form at that. The warrior is a figure for the sovereign force of black metal, the closest related idea to which is clearly Bataille's concept of sovereignty which designates exactly that which is heterogeneous to the sovereign function denoted by *justitium*, the sacralization of power (and of mastery), whether in the symbol or the body of the legislator-king. As Denis Hollier states, Bataille's concept of sovereignty corresponds to something that is much nearer 'to the noncontractual liberty which is congenital with the warrior function'.

> For the warrior has nothing to do with what one understands as a soldier or that Roman invention, 'the military man'. Even when he is not the only one to be fighting, a warrior always fights alone: the solitary hero of single combats. And he fights for fighting's sake, carried away by heroic fury. For the prestige of risk. Fundamentally undisciplined, he is the inspired warrior of the joust, the *vates* of the field of battle who, like Plato's poet, can fight only as one possessed, transported. (Hollier, 1988, 39)

And it is precisely in that poetic or musical movement of transportation that the sovereign aspect emerges as 'the object dissolves into NOTHING' (Bataille, 1991, 204); neither symbol nor living law, but the evanescent movement between sound and silence in the space-time between life and death in which music is sovereign. As Jacques Derrida, following Bataille, affirms, 'simultaneously more and less a lordship than lordship, sovereignty is totally other' (Derrida, 1986, 256). Hence, Darkthrone, Beherit, Gorgoroth, and all the other names for Lucifer and Satan that star the black metal firmament; and hence, perhaps above all, Mayhem. All are fictional names for the sovereign aspect that will serve no master and that refuses all forms of subordination. Neither force of law nor originary violence, the sovereign impulse is essential to any mode of rebellion, any breaching of closed systems, any process of transformation political or personal.

It is moreover only through actualizing this sovereign aspect that one might bring to bear the forces of black metal to the realization of one's own powers. And this has absolutely nothing to do with individualism, mastery, subordination and so on. 'Although I scorn the completely modern idea of "a self-made man", as a Luciferist I solemnly hold up the view that man must reach as far as one can with his own powers' (IC Rex, in Ulvhel, 2009). To where does one reach, what use are these powers? Such questions simply return us back to the ground on which we grovel 'in the concatenation of useful activity' (Bataille, 1991, 203). Answers cannot be anticipated, future effects cannot be known since knowledge is always the result of work; 'it is always a servile operation, indefinitely resumed, indefinitely repeated' (202). It is impossible for knowledge to be sovereign; it would have to occur in a moment. But the moment remains outside, short of or beyond, all knowledge' (202). And yet, it is just such knowledge of the moment that is impossibly both inside and outside itself that is promised, paradoxically, in the black metal philosophorum of hideous gnosis.

3. Philosophorum

> At long last, did one not have to sacrifice for once whatever is comforting, holy, healing; all hope, all faith in hidden harmony, in future blisses and justices? Didn't one have to sacrifice God himself?
> Friedrich Nietzsche (1966, 585)

> Welcome to my sacrifice
> Bathory, 'Sacrifice' (1984)

By knowledge I do not just mean the knowledge produced through the work of philosophy or academic discourse, or discourse per se, that is, the locus of a social bond; nor am I referring simply to the esoteric knowledge located in arcane texts and objects; nor do I mean the *savoir faire*, the know-how, of the musicians, the in-competence that produces black metal's magnificent yet hellish racket. All of these are important, and one can see that in so far as black metal is an effect of discourse, it is a discourse that exacerbates the problem of the social bond through refusing comprehensibility by excoriating voice and language in sonic aggression. Yet it is precisely through such sonic ascesis that the social bond is negatively sustained. Music, after all, is nothing but social bond, establishing a community of listeners somewhere that can perceive, and as such become bound by, a particular organization of sound. Otherwise music is no different from the indifferent howling of the wind that black metal seeks to evoke, but always for somebody, if only just for oneself, to place oneself at the very limit of oneself where one is dissolved to NOTHING. This is the *a*music of black metal: 'my feelings already enclose me as in a tomb and yet, above me, I imagine a song similar to the modulation of light, from cloud to cloud . . . in the unbearable expanse of the skies . . . How can I avoid the intimate, never-ending, horror of being? . . . This heart crying a thousand tender joys, how can I fail to open it to the void?' (Bataille, 2001, 11)

Rather, the blackened knowledge that I wish to invoke is, as the title of this symposium suggests, hideous gnosis. This gnosis, like any gnosis hideous or not, is starred by the truth that is revealed through the work of intuition or of an 'instinctive' knowledge; that is to say, a knowledge that doesn't know how it knows or even that it knows. 'My music does not come from a philosophy but from a pre-critical compulsion, an instinct which comes prior to the thought and does not depend on it . . . The negativity of my sound is simply the representation of my most hidden emotions' (Ovskum, in Ulvhel, 2009). Given that this so-called instinct 'comes' in the form of music, it should more accurately be called a drive. An instinct (alimentary or sexual, say) that does not have a direct relation to its object but is mediated or shaped by a symbolic form is called a drive. And a drive has an indirect relation to its object, which is to say that it circulates it. In the case of music and song this is the invocatory drive, a designation of course particularly appropriate to black metal which perhaps consists entirely as an invocation: calling on God in order to contemplate and exult in the torment of his extinction, or the invocation of Satan in the conjuring-up of evil, that which will not serve.

In so far as it was harnessed and articulated by language, 'Freud considered the drive to be structured like a montage' (Lacan, 2005, 718). In black metal, the invocatory drive is articulated by the music to form the martial/amorous lamella-armour of the warrior decked in metal plates, spikes and bullet belts that is darkly erotic in the sense of being *jenseits* (beyond, the other side of, the dark side of) the *lustprinzips*, the pleasure principle. The lamellar armour of the drive forms an intensive surface that extends the organism (the voice) 'to its true limit, which goes further than the body's limit' (Lacan, 2005, 719), establishing its territory in and as the sound that unfolds an abyssal darkness into which the voice qua voice fades away. The unanswerable invocation reveals the deadly meaning of the lamella in the sense that the only meaning is the meaning of death. The prosthetic armour may for a while offer a semblance of protection, of existence, but its presence signifies only the vulnerability and inevitable death of the organism that it brings into battle. It is of course the armour, the weapons, the metal not the organism that actually contests the battle. Sound, that always refers back to an originary dissonance, that is always the sound of the elemental war for existence, kills even at the moment that it heralds the coming of death and silence. 'This is why every drive is virtually a death drive' (Lacan, 2005, 719).

Invocation requires ritual and in black metal that ritual is sacrifice: 'At long last, did one not have to sacrifice for once whatever is comforting, holy, healing; all hope, all faith in hidden harmony, in future blisses and justices? Didn't one have to sacrifice God himself?' (Friedrich Nietzsche). Along with God is sacrificed his representative, 'welcome to my sacrifice' (Bathory), the subject of faith and knowledge, discourse and speech at the attenuated limits of a voice become mere breath that is always the last breath expiring in the sovereign space between life and death. The object of subjectifying power is sacrificed, evacuated, but as such the void that is disclosed is rendered divine. Sacrifice makes sacred, opening up divine inexistence. Circulating the hole, black metal silences the voice in the midst of its hellish racket as it becomes pure sonic drive, nothing but a corpse-painted lamella, an undead tessellated sound-surface, metallic last-breath death rattle.

Hideous gnosis, the in-competence of an *a*musical death drive, which loses itself, dissipates itself at the site of nonknowledge marked by the name of death in the crucible of metalorical transformations.

4. Metaloricum

> I myself am in a world I recognize as profoundly inaccessible to me.
> Georges Bataille (2001, 113).

> Faded am I, behind a wall of consciousness / Still feeling a different World / Surrounding Me.
> Darkthrone, 'Paragon Belial' (1992).

Certainly it is vain for theory to aspire to the condition of black metal, just as it would be for theory to aspire to the condition of any music at all. Even so, such an aspiration is familiar from Western philosophical theory generally, at least since Romanticism, wherein music is attributed with meaning and significance beyond language, an attribution precisely correlated to the degree to which music is also regarded as deficient, purely imaginary, devoid of theory, vehicle of base emotions and so on. What devilish alchemy is this that turns base material into sonic gold only for it to turn to shit as the goat glances in the mirror? Oh black Narcissus, the exquisite horror of self-reflection! Black metal has no meaning, of course—but then neither does any music—even as it opens up, in the non-sense, the excess of meaning that it evokes, the domain of non-knowledge.

Black metal theory is *forged* through the process of its 'tools' being placed in the icy furnace of blackened affinities and affections, giving itself over to the power of modification to which black metal is itself an effect, heterogeneous no doubt, but one that opens onto the same Night. Let us say that black metal theory cannot know—can never know—its object: the black metal that rings out in the impenetrable darkness of its so-called intellectual emptiness. Like an object sovereign in its exteriority, an object that is precisely not a thing—a thing for us—such an object would be God; that is to say the God that black metal invokes in order to banish Him, the God that sits, perpetually exchanging places with Satan, at the mediating position between the possible and the impossible.

Black metal, for some, for a few, provides the locus of this inaccessibility, provides the experience of *non-knowledge* that communicates ecstasy, that is to say places someone at the limit of being in a radical questioning of being itself. This questioning occurs in and as an inchoate experience that nevertheless provides the (groundless) ground of self-reflection in a speculation that reflects, interminably, on the im-possibility of indefinite and limitless being.

Kathaarian Life Code of Non-Knowledge

1. 'The Triumph of chaos—Has Guided our Path / we Circle the holy Sinai'. Black metal blackening thought blackening metal blackening theory . . . Like the circularity of the spectral drive that invokes God simply in order to exorcise Him from the vast

nocturnal landscape that his death discloses. Black metal theory is circular; circular theory is the only plausible theory. 'To be of one's time is quite simply to be a stooge' (Bataille, 2001, 107), the exploited dupe of slavish exigencies.
2. Circular theory must begin, which is to say continue, not from a proposition but from the blackness that precedes it, just as it culminates, which is to say begins, in the blackened knowledge that is non-knowledge. 'A strong light—the only Night'.
3. Black metal glints in sparks mixed with Coyote eyes and resonates in shortened cycles which black metal theory can only describe, knowledge fired across the desertified landscape; instances of the nonknowledge of the moment.
4. 'Face of the goat in the mirror': the horror of self-reflexive nonrecognition discloses the black metal Baphomet, 'Baphomet in steel', the prince of modifications: 'I entered the soul of the snake', the one, no doubt, that consumed itself in a blaze of icy fire.
5. The dis-identification of Satan and the death of God, of the erotic and the laughable, the stupid and the playful, the poetic and the *a*musical, with the unknown is the key to all theoretical difficulties. Recognizing its worthlessness, its good-for-nothingness, theoretical knowledge returns with the dream of making its own God, a Paragon Belial, the sum and sublimation of all earthly insufficiencies. And yet . . .
6. The substitution of absolute dissatisfaction, the invisible force of an abyssic hatred, for relative

insufficiencies results in the passage from insubordination to sovereignty in a blasphemous cyclone of infernal in-difference, stirring in the metalorical furnace . . .
7. The final nature of dissatisfaction is the truth of awakening:
   For this Eternal Winter
   A New God Ruled the Sky
   The Million Hands Of Joy
   Have something holy to Burn

A new God is invoked but only for the joy of again consuming Him in flames, for igniting the divine in-existence in a blaze in the Northern sky.

5. Baphomet

All the gods died of laughter to hear one among them proclaim himself unique!
     Pierre Klossowski, *The Baphomet* (1988, 111)

Baphomet in Steel / For the Flesh of Cain / A Throne made by remains / of 12 holy Disciples
     Darkthrone, 'Kathaarian Life Code', (1992)

The disembodied soul of Øysten Aarseth, exhaled in his last dying breath and born on the icy winter wind, howled through the window of an old house outside Oslo. Dead lay there, still dead, half of his head pressed up against the wood panelling, his knife and shotgun by his side, the floor splattered with dried blood and brain matter. Suspended in time, Dead's last exhaled breath picked off the last few layers of blasted skull and scooped out the putrefying tissue to disclose another head made of gold. A metalhead.

Aarseth was returned to his final state, on the day of his fatal stabbing. As the new golden-headed Dead seemingly arose from the dead, Aarseth got down on his knees before the strange goatlike yet godly creature, 'My saviour!' he stammered.

'Why do you call me saviour and kneel to me like a God' said Dead, 'I am not a creator who enslaves being to what he creates, what he creates to a single self, and this self to a single body. Øysten, the millions of selves that you oppress within yourself are dead and have resurrected millions of times in you, unbeknownst to your single self'.

'Is it not myself that you have rescued from the knife of Vikernes?'

'In the suspension of historical time, events echo throughout infinity and individuals eternally. But everything a breath has perpetrated through its body can remain without consequence once it has left its body, since we differ in no wise from the winds of air currents, even when they bring malice or sensual craving to infect other places. I am here to serve you'.

'What greater service could you ever perform for me than to give me back to myself!'

'To free you from yourself . . . '

At this point a chill entered the room as the already-dead breath of Varg Vikernes merged with the breath of his victim, finding himself much weaker than the latter as he quickly sought to separate. Greeted with no sense of moral atonement, Vikernes was struck by a violence of another order to the one he perpetrated: one of total indifference, the worst kind of violence, an indifference that left no trace (108).

'From myself?' Continued Aarseth, 'Is it not necessary that I be judged in my body?'

'It is not necessary', said Dead's golden head, and explained that, on the contrary, the Judgement of God had been infinitely suspended since He became consumed in flames. 'Henceforth humankind has changed in substance: it can be no more damned than saved'. Consequently, with this interruption of Divine presence and authority, the entire order of theological judgement and value is overturned (see James, 2005). In this atemporal space, as fallen souls follow the freezing moon, memories of the past are revived as momentary states of intensity, which, without identity or propriety, are exchangeable from soul to soul. 'Here is no peace made of human flesh' said Dead and prepared himself to breeze through the leaves of the forest.

'You're leaving me? Stop', Aarseth begged. 'By what name may I invoke you?'

'You refuse my services! What does my name matter to you? In truth I tell you: the millions of brothers and sisters inside you, who have died for your high idea of yourself—Euronymous!—know my name well, and are reborn in it; no proper name exists for the hyperbolic breath that is my own, anymore than anyone's high idea of himself can resist the vertigo of my great height; my forehead dominates the stars and my feet stir the abysses of the universe'.

'Spell it for me, I beg you, so I will have invoked you but once!'

Dead began:

'B-A . . .'

'Ba . . . ?' repeated Euronymous.

'P-H-O . . .' continued Dead.

'. . . pho . . . ?'

'M-E-T . . .'

'. . . Met! . . .' (Klossowski, 1988, 99)

Baphomet, otherwise known as Prince of Modifications, opposed to the Christian principle that guarantees the identity of the soul and the unity of being. To quote Pierre Klossowski, '*Ba*silieus philoso*pho*rum *mét*allicorum: the sovereign of metallurgical philosophers, precursors of black metal theorists, that is, of the alchemical laboratories that were supposedly established in various chapters of the knights Templar' (1988, 165). 'The Prince of Modifications overturns all identity and absorbs being into the principle of radical multiplicity', that is to say into the principle of blackness (James, 2005, 126).

The antichrist, in the form of an anteater affirms that '*When one god proclaimed himself unique, all the other gods died of laughter!*' Reborn in the breath of this laughter the million godlike hands find themselves again with something holy to burn, as the black metal circle turns eternally in a clamour for being that unfolds a process of becoming as infinite non-self-identical multiplicity beyond all figures of unity or of the One. 'Anything can happen', said Dead, 'in the infinite blackening of the universe'.

'Be faithful to your oblivion!' (Klossowski, 1988, 101).

Kingston University, London

References

Giorgio Agamben (2005) *State of Exception*, Chicago: University of Chicago Press.

Georges Bataille (1991) *The Accursed Share* II and III, trans. Robert Hurley, New York: Zone Books.

Georges Bataille (2001) *The Unfinished System of Nonknowledge* ed. Stuart Kendall, Minneapolis: University of Minnesota Press.

Gilles Deleuze (1995) *Negotiations*. NY: Columbia University

Press.
Jacques Derrida (1986) *Writing and Difference*. London: Routledge.
Michel Foucault (1986) *Language, Counter-Memory, Practice*. translated by Donald Bouchard, Ithaca: Cornell University Press.
Michel Foucault (1988) *Politics, Philosophy, Culture* edited by Lawrence D. Kritzman, London: Routledge.
Denis Hollier (1988) 'January 21st' *Stanford French Review* XII, 1 (Spring), pp. 31-47, 39.
Keith Kahn-Harris (2007) *Extreme Metal: Music and Culture on the Edge*. London: Berg.
Pierre Klossowski (1988) *The Baphomet* translated by Sophie Hawkes and Stephen Sartorelli, Colorado: Eridanos Press.
Ian James (2005) 'Evaluating Klossowski's *Le Baphomet*', *diacritics* (35. 1, Spring), 119-135.
Jacques Lacan (2005) *Écrits* translated by Bruce Fink, NY: WW Norton.
Friedrich Nietzsche (1966) *Beyond Good and Evil* translated by Walter Kaufman. NY: Random House.
Brandon Stousy (2008) *Show No Mercy* (5/24/08) <http://www.pitchforkmedia.com/article/feature/50777-column-show-no-mercy>
Ulvhel (2009) <http://ulvhel.110mb.com/ulvhel6>

Discography
Bathory (1984) *Bathory*. Black Mark.
Darkthrone (1992) *A Blaze in the Northern Sky*. Peaceville.
Emperor (1997), *Anthems to the Welkin at Dusk*. Candlelight Records.
Mayhem (1994) *De Mysteriis Dom Sathanas*. Deathlike Silence.

TRANSCENDENTAL BLACK METAL

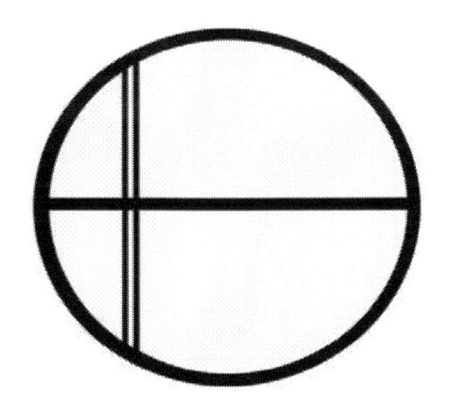

A VISION OF APOCALYPTIC HUMANISM

BY

HUNTER HUNT-HENDRIX

PROLEGOMENON

One could propose a new meaning for black metal along with a new array of techniques to activate that meaning. The meaning of Transcendental Black Metal is Affirmation, and its new technique is the Burst Beat.

The will to power has two stages. The first may be called Fortification; the establishment of a paradigm or set of rules and the ensuing exploration of potential that lies within those constraints. The second stage may be termed Sacrifice; an auto-destruction, a self-overcoming whereby the initial rules, having been fully digested and satisfied, are thereby mutilated. They are transformed into the basis for something new and unprecedented.

Transcendental Black Metal is black metal in the mode of Sacrifice. It is a clearing aside of contingent features and a fresh exploration of the essence of black metal. As such it is solar, hypertrophic, courageous, finite and penultimate. Its tone is Affirmation and its key technique is the Burst Beat.

The black metal that was born in Scandinavia in the mode of Fortification can be termed Hyperborean Black Metal. Hyperborean Black Metal is lunar, atrophic, depraved, infinite and pure. The symbol of its birth is the Death of Dead. Its tone is Nihilism and its key technique is the Blast Beat.

Today USBM stands in the shadow of Hyperborean Black Metal. The time has come for a decisive break with the European tradition and the establishment of a truly American black metal. And we should say "American" rather than "US": the US is a declining empire; America is an eternal ideal representing human dignity, hybridization and creative evolution.

The act of renihilation is the betrayal of Hyperborean Black Metal and an affirmation of Transcendental Black Metal. And it is at the same time the constitution of an apocalyptic humanism to be termed Aesthethics. As such, the question of Transcendental Black Metal is only the tip of an iceberg at the base of which is hidden a new relationship between art, politics, ethics and religion.

PART I
THE DEATH OF DEAD

THE HAPTIC VOID AS FINAL CAUSE

The history of metal can be considered in terms of levels of intensity. Considered in this way, black metal shows itself to be a culmination or endpoint of this history, and also a dead end.

The historical development of extreme metal is not a chance series of stylistic shifts. It is teleological - governed by a dimly understood but acutely felt Ideal, or a final cause. This final cause is named the Haptic Void.

The Haptic Void is a hypothetical total or maximal level of intensity. It is the horizon of the history of metal.

Orientation towards the Haptic Void is expressed as feeling. The feeling is a unity, but in thought we can break it down into four elements:

There is first of all a certain muscular clenching, a constriction of the jaws, fists, arms and chest.
Secondarily there is an affect: a certain aggression or brutality, a paradoxical sense of power, destruction, fullness and emptiness.
Thirdly it features a primordial satisfaction relating to the affect which acts normatively. Good metal produces a satisfying bouquet of clenching, constriction and brutal affect.
Finally there is a barely discernable *je ne sais quoi* that says "not enough". A complementary dissatisfaction – as though no brutal breakdown can be quite brutal enough. It is a fissure, a crack, a lack of being. An insufficiency compared to the promised plenitude. Maybe it's the inability of any concrete song to measure up to the inspiration that gave birth to it. Paradoxically this dissatisfaction is felt in direct proportion to the level of its complement.

It is this dissatisfaction, this fourth element, which causes extreme metal to develop new styles over time. This is the pull of the final cause. This opening, this fissure, is the angel that guides metal's history. We see metal march towards the void, leaving thrash, death metal and black metal, successively, in its wake.

But the promise made by the Haptic Void is a lie. Only its absence is ever present.

TRANSILVANIAN HUNGER

Hyperborean Black Metal is the culmination of the history of extreme metal. Hyperborean Black Metal was born in the

Arctic Circle, which is traditionally known as the Hyperborean realm. The Hyperborean realm is a land that is fallow because it lacks periodicity. There is no birth or death there because the sun neither rises nor sets.

Hyperborean Black Metal is the culmination of the history of extreme metal (which is itself the culmination of the history of the Death of God). The subject of this history may be compared to a mountaineer, maneuvering over and across the various terrains of thrash, grindcore and death metal – or rather, carving these terrains into the mountainside - and striving to reach the Haptic Void, dimly understood but strongly felt, glimmering brightly at the summit.

Hyperborean Black Metal represents the moutaineer's arrival at the peak and a supposed leap off of it, directly into the Haptic Void. A total, maximal intensity. A complete flood of sound. An absolute plenitude.

But there he learns that totality is indistinguishable from nothingness. He learns that it is impossible to leap into the horizon. And he is left, crestfallen, frozen and alone, in the Hyperborean realm. It is a dead static place, a polar land where there is no oscillation between day and night. But stasis is atrophy. The Hyperborean realm is dead with purity, totally absolute, selfsame and eternal. The mountaineer undergoes a profound apostasy that he cannot fully understand and arrives at nihilism.

The technique of Hyperborean Black Metal is the blast beat. Pure black metal, represented by Transilvanian Hunger, means continuous open strumming and a continuous blast beat. But the pure blast beat is eternity in itself. No articulated figures, no beginning, no end, no pauses, no dynamic range. It is a bird soaring in the air with nowhere to perch even for a moment. What seemed at first to be a great clamor dwindles to an atrophied hum. Having climbed to the peak of the mountain, the mountaineer lies down and freezes to death.

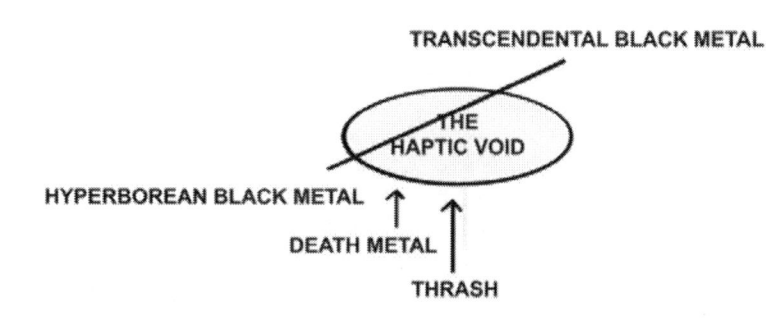

```
                          TRANSCENDENTAL BLACK METAL
                                    /
                            ( THE  /    )
                            ( HAPTIC VOID )
   HYPERBOREAN BLACK METAL  ↑
                   DEATH METAL ↑
                          THRASH
```

PART II
THE AFFIRMATION OF AFFIRMATION

AMERICA

Transcendental Black Metal represents a new relationship to the Haptic Void and the self-overcoming of Hyperborean Black Metal. It is a sublimation of Hyperborean Black Metal in both its spiritual aspect and its technical aspect. Spiritually, it transforms Nihilism into Affirmation. Technically, it transforms the Blast Beat into the Burst Beat.

Spiritually we acknowledge Nihilism, and we refuse to sink into it, impossible as the task may be. Transcendental Black Metal is a Renihilation, a "No" to the entire array of

Negations, which turns to an affirmation of the continuity of all things.

Transcendental Black Metal is the reanimation of the form of black metal with a new soul, a soul full of chaos, frenzy and ecstasy. A specifically American joyful clamor which is also a tremor. Or maybe it is the opposite act: a peeling away of the husk of convention, the dead skin of clichés and a fresh exploration of the living soul of black metal, with the aim to reactivate its purest essence and produce something that grows from it but does not resemble its earlier incarnations because it is built from the ground up in a different time and place. Built in America. An America that has never existed and may never exist. The America that represents the apocalyptic humanism of William Blake. The America celebrated by Aaron Copeland's Appalachian Spring or Ornette Coleman's Skies of America.

This America is a metaphor for pure unrestricted creativity, the courageous exercise of will and the joyful experience of the continuity of existence. A celebration of the hybrid and of creative evolution.

THE BURST BEAT

The backbone of Transcendental Black metal is the Burst Beat. The burst beat is a hyper blast beat, a blast beat that ebbs, flows, expands and contracts, breaths. It replaces death and atrophy with life and hypertrophy. This transformation is accomplished by two features: acceleration and rupture.

The first feature of the burst beat is acceleration. The burst beat accelerates and decelerates. It has an ebb and a flow. This flow both mirrors life and stimulates life. It expands and contracts like the tide, the economy, day and night, inhalation and exhalation, life and death.

The second feature of the burst beat is rupture. The burst beat features sudden ruptures or phase transitions. Just like all natural systems, it breaks suddenly from one state to another. Consider the horse as it switches from walk to trot to canter. Consider water as it switches from ice to liquid to gas. The moment of the rupture is the moment of transcendence. What is holy if not the moment that water turns to steam? Or the moment that a walk turns to a run?

The burst beat expresses an arc of intensity. It responds to and supplements the melodic flow rather than providing a rhythmic container or backdrop. The rate of change of the tempo, whether positive or negative, corresponds to a level of intensity. Any static tempo is a zero degree.

The burst requires total expenditure of power and its very exercise fosters growth and increase of strength. And yet the burst beat never arrives anywhere, eternally "not yet" at its destination, eternally "almost" at the target tempo. Like a nomad, the burst beat knows it will never arrive.

By mirroring life, the burst beat stimulates and fosters life. By fostering life, Transcendental Black Metal affirms life.

HYPERBOREAN	TRANSCENDENTAL
NIHILISM	AFFIRMATION
ATROPHY	HYPERTROPHY
BLAST BEAT	BURST BEAT
LUNAR	SOLAR
DEPRAVITY	COURAGE
THE INFINITE	THE FINITE
PURITY	PENULTIMACY

PROPERTIES

Transcendental Black Metal exists as a unity, but in thought it can be analyzed into seven properties.

Why is Transcendental Black Metal affirmative?

Transcendental Black Metal is in fact nihilism, however it is a double nihilism and a final nihilism, a once and for all negation of the entire series of negations. With this final "No" we arrive a sort of vertiginous Affirmation, an Affirmation that is white-knuckled, terrified, unsentimental, and courageous. What we affirm is the facticity of time and the undecidability of the future. Our affirmation is a refusal to deny.

Why is Transcendental Black Metal hypertrophic?

Growth is life, stasis is decay. We are committed to striving eternally, living a sort of permanent revolution. Just as a well exercised muscle is beautiful and powerful, so we will be beautiful and powerful. In truth, there is no stasis. The only choice is between atrophy and hypertrophy. The celebration of atrophy is confused, weak, and neurotic. The celebration of hypertrophy is honest and alive.

Why is Transcendental Black Metal solar?

Transcendental black metal is solar in three respects, following three aspects of the sun: periodicity, intensity and honesty. The sun lets things be born and grow, so that they may die. The burst beat is periodic because is rises and sets like the sun. The sun mesmerizes and burns. We participate in intensity because we are not sentimental and we know that death comes. But why not follow a goal, follow the sun and chase after its flairs? Why not go up in flames rather than dwindle to a speck of sand? The sun represents Truth and reveals all that it touches. We are honest because we refuse to lurk in the shadows, we refuse to point fingers, we refuse to perform our rites in secret. We are not sickly, spiteful, hateful. We do not hide behind costumes or esoterica.

Why do we revere the finite rather than the infinite?

What is sacred is the taking of each concrete step. Each honest decision. The infinite is obvious and everywhere. To engage the finite takes courage and produces hypertrophy. God is infinite, nature is infinite. The infinite is everywhere and cheap. It is the finite that is rare. It is the finite that is peculiar to humankind. Finitude means confronting what is present at hand authentically and doing what is honest with the means one has at one's disposal. The solar nourishes the finite. The finite is born, strives, and dies.

Why do we revere penultimacy?

Transcendental black metal sacralizes the penultimate moment, the "almost" or the "not yet", because it has been found that *there is nothing after the penultimate moment*. The penultimate moment is the final moment, and it takes place at every moment. The fabric of existence is open. There is nothing that is complete; there is nothing that is pure.

Why is Transcendental Black Metal courageous?

Courage is open and raw. Courage means flying towards the horizon with no guarantee of a place to land. Courage is the active, honest leap from one moment to the next. No dissimulation, no excuses, no irony, no complaints. Courage has no object of attack. Courage is not jaded, disappointed, disaffected. Courage is not a flight into fantasy or nostalgia. It is the opposite of Depravity. Depravity is false freedom. A poison dart shot from the shadows. A retreat that seems like an advance. An attack that is really only a shield. Depravity is dissimulation; courage is authenticity. Courage has no image of itself. It is trailblazing. It has no path before it. Its only trace is the wake it leaves behind.

EPILOGUE
SEVEN THESES ON AESTHETHICS

1. Black Metal represents the self-overcoming of Counterculture and the rise of Aesthethics

2. The Aesthethic could be a third modality of art alongside the comic and the tragic. Neither saccharine nor ironic, concerned neither with ineffable truth nor the all-too-obvious. It would be a directly neural art fostering joy, health, resonance, awakening, transfiguration and courage.

3. The Aesthethic is aesthetic, ascetic and ethical

4. The ancients identified the True, the Good and the Beautiful. After the dust settles, and the work of modernity and postmodernity is done, and the divisions between high culture, mass culture and counterculture have been obliterated, what is left? A single, shining Culture which is True, Good, and Beautiful.

5. In the age of information culture has traveled down from the superstructure into the base. Stripped of coercive power long ago, culture has now been granted unprecedented economic force, which enhances its spiritual power, power over minds and hearts. The question remains of what its function should be.

6. The murder of Euronymous by Varg Vikernes appears as the founding gesture of the tradition of black metal. In fact, it is a mere origin myth, foreclosing the real founding gesture. The real gesture, though it is less notorious, is the suicide of Dead. Compare Cobain "I betrayed the counterculture" to Dead, "I betrayed myself to the counterculture". Dead's death secretly inaugurates the birth of black metal and the death of counterculture as such. Just as the absence of Dead's voice haunts De Mysteriis, so Attila's recent return to Mayhem signifies that we are ready to explore the implications of Dead's suicide.

7. Aesthethics is a resurrection of the aura and an affirmation of the power of meaning to mean.

ANTI-COSMOSIS: BLACK MAHAPRALAYA
Nicola Masciandaro

God or the good or the place does not take place, but is the taking-place [*aver-luogo*] of the entities, their innermost exteriority.

–Giorgio Agamben[2]

---

[1] Arizmenda, *Within the Vacuum of Infinity . . .* (Dismal Cursings, 2009). See *Begotten*, dir. E. Elias Merhige (1991), 38th minute.

> I don't want to be where I am, or anywhere for that matter.
> —Malefic of Xasthur[3]

The very questions "Whence?" and "Whither?" presuppose the beginning and end of this evolving creation. *The beginning of evolution is the beginning of time and the end of evolution is the end of time.* Evolution has both beginning and end because time has both beginning and end. Between the beginning and the end of this changing world there are many cycles, but there is, in and through these cycles, a continuity of cosmic evolution. The real termination of the evolutionary process is called *Mahapralaya* or the final annihilation of the world, when the world becomes what it was in the beginning, namely *nothing*. . . . Just as the varied world of experience completely disappears for the man who is in deep sleep, the entire objective cosmos which is the creation of *Maya* vanishes into nothingness at the time of *Mahapralaya*. It is as if the universe had never existed at all. Even during the evolutionary period the universe is in itself nothing but imagination. There is in fact only one indivisible and eternal Reality and it has neither beginning nor end. It is beyond time. From the point of view of this timeless Reality the whole time-process is purely imaginary, and billions of years which have passed and billions of years

---

[2] Giorgio Agamben, *The Coming Community*. trans. Michael Hardt (Minneapolis: University of Minnesota Press, 1993), 14

[3] "Interview: Xasthur," <http://www.anus.com/metal/about/interviews/xasthur/>.

which are to pass do not have even the value of a second. It is as if they had not existed at all.

—Meher Baba[4]

There is gangrene in the tubes / Of the vermicular ethics of how / Your world view presents itself / Contradictions in terms of how / Your life evolves in the chain of being / I claim you were never a part of reality

—Mayhem[5]

One bright Sunday, as he was sitting withdrawn and deep in thought, there came to him in the calmness of his mind the figure of a rational being who was sophisticated in speech but inexperienced in deeds and who overflowed with rich ostentation. He began speaking to the figure thus: Where do you come from? It said: I never came from anywhere. He said: Tell me, what are you? It said: I am nothing. He said: What do you want? It answered and said: I want nothing. And he said: This is very strange. Tell me, what is your name? It said: I am called nameless wild one. The *disciple* said: You are well named "the wild one" because your words and answers are completely wild. Now tell me something I shall ask you. Where does your wisdom take you? It said: to unrestrained liberty.

—Henry of Suso[6]

---

[4] Meher Baba, *Discourses*, I.45-6.
[5] "Chimera," *Chimera* (Season of Mist, 2004).
[6] Hentry of Suso, *The Little Book of Truth*, Chapter 6, cited from *Henry Suso: The Exemplar, with Two German Sermons*, ed. and trans. Frank Tobin (Mahwah, NJ: Paulist Press, 1989), 326.

I pick up the guitar play until I found a riff that makes me either shudder in fear, cry with pain, tremble with anger and I will play that riff many times over... I am never content or never will be with the restrictions set upon me. I will destroy cosmos and return to freedom!
—Donn of Teutoburg Forest[7]

I contest in the name of contestation what experience itself is (the will to proceed to the end of the possible). Experience, its authority, its method, do not distinguish themselves from the contestation.
—Georges Bataille[8]

We are the Circle of Black Twilight. Spreading Kaos and Dissonance through sacred ceremonial worship. We have transcended from this mind and flesh. We exist within this darkness and dwell within it's unending void of disharmony. You too will come to proclaim it's ultimate presence. [*sic*]
—Volahn[9]

A *catena* is a medieval form of exegetical commentary composed wholly of a *chain* of citations from other works. Representing textual significance as a plenitude spanning the voices of multiple authors, the textual form, exemplified by

---

[7] "Interview with Teutoburg Forest," <http://blogs.myspace.com/usbmsarchives>.

[8] *Inner Experience*, trans. Leslie Anne Boldt (Albany: State University of New York Press, 1988), 12.

[9] Cited from Crepúsculo Negro pamphlet (128 of 400).

Aquinas's *Catena Aurea* on the four gospels, is the generic analogue of the cosmic spectacle that held sway during the thousand years or so when *catenae* were written, namely, the vision of the universe as constituting a great chain of being, an ordered procession of entities formally bound together via the unity of their common origin and end. As Macrobius explains, with properly consequential syntax, in his *Commentary on the Dream of Scipio*:

> since Mind emanates from the Supreme God, and Soul from Mind, and Mind, indeed, forms and suffuses all below with life, and since this is the one splendor lighting up everything and visible in all, like a countenance reflected in many mirrors arranged in a row, and since all follow on in continuous succession, degenerating step by step [*degenerantia per ordinem*] in their downward course, the close observer will find that from the Supreme God even to the bottommost dregs of the universe [*a summo deo usque ad ultimam rerum faecem*] there is one tie [*conexio*], binding at every link and never broken. This is the golden chain [*catena aurea*] of Homer which, he tells us, God ordered to hang down from the sky to the earth.[10]

The chain principle is an ontological wholism. It threads the fact of universe itself, expressing the inseparability of the *what* and the *that*.[11] The cosmic *catena* is the necessary point of identity,

---

[10] Macrobius, *Commentary on the Dream of Scipio*, trans. William Harris Stahl (New York: Columbia University Press, 1952), 14.15.

[11] "The distinction does not happen to us arbitrarily or from time to time, but *fundamentally* and constantly. . . . For precisely in order to

piercing every entity, between essence and existence, the invisible thing making it so that everything is next to something else and part of everything itself. It is thus in a full and total

mahapralaya

12

sense the *chain of being*, the fact of being's being a chain or binding: at once the universal necessity of the actuality of the

---

experience *what* and *how* beings in each case *are* in themselves as the beings that they *are*, we must—although not conceptually—already understand something like the what-being [*Was-sein*] and the that-being [*Dass-sein*] of beings. . . . We never ever experience anything about being subsequently or after the event from beings; rather beings—wherever and however we approach them—*already* stand *in the light of being*. In the metaphysical sense, therefore, the distinction stands at the commencement of Dasein itself. . . . Man, therefore, always has the possibility of asking: What is that? And Is it at all or is it not?" (Martin Heidegger, *The Fundamental Concepts of Metaphysics: World, Finitude, Solitude*, trans. William McNeill and Nicholas Walker [Bloomington: Indiana University Press, 1995], 357.)

[12] Mahapralaya, *Hän joka on nielevä ajan* (Demo, 2007)

everything (the fact that there is such a thing as everything) and the individual necessity of the actuality of individuation (the fact that each thing is inexorably shackled to itself).[13] The chain encompasses from within the impossible unity of perspective on being that cosmos presupposes: the definite vision of the unbounded whole from the position of one-sided asymmetry occupied by the individual.

I begin with a *catena*, really an acatena—a broken, scriptureless exegetical chain—as the only conceivable way of opening discourse on anti-cosmic black metal, an art that proceeds in principle against the universe as the principle of order, which is what *cosmos* means, and thus against the very possibility or ground of discourse. We may recall that *discourse*, which signifies *logos* as a circulation between beings (*dis-cursus*),

---

[13] "Why am I me? A stupid question. . . . I am too stupid to answer this question. And to ask it, just stupid enough. What is the mechanism of such stupid questioning? I imagine a small organ, neither inside nor outside myself, like a polymelic phantom limb, a subtle psychic appendage implanted at birth behind my crown, during the moment of my coming to be, whenever that was. This organ (or appendix, or tumor), whose painful inflammation is despair—'despair is the paroxysm of individuation' (Cioran)—is like a strange supplementary bodily member, intimate and inessential, which I can feel yet not move, barely move yet without feeling. Stupid organ, organ of stupidity. It moves, is moved, like an inalienable shackle, only to reinforce its immobility. Am I to sever this organ, hemorrhage of haecceity, escape it? '[E]scape is the need to get out of oneself, that is, *to break that most radical and unalterably binding of chains, the fact that the I [moi] is oneself [soi-mếme]*' (Levinas). Just *who*, then, would escape?" (Nicola Masciandaro, "Individuation: This Stupidity," *Postmedieval* 1 [2010], forthcoming). "The act whereby being—existence—is bestowed upon us is an *unbearable* surpassing of being" (Bataille).

implies an immanence/emergence of order, the actualization of a shared reality as its medium. Only thus does word result in *text* (fr. *texere*, to weave), the higher order fabric (cf. "fabric of the universe") produced when the thread of language passes to and fro across itself. Fulfilling such a discursive ontology on a cosmic scale, Dante's *Commedia* realizes itself in the joyful retelling of a vision of a complex universal form that takes a codexical, self-bound shape:

> In its depth I saw ingathered, bound by love in one single volume, that which is dispersed in leaves throughout the universe: substances and accidents and their relations, as though fused together in such a way that what I tell is but a simple light. The universal form of this knot I believe that I saw, because, in telling this, I feel my joy increase.[14]

Inside the anticosmic impulse, the reality of such a volume, and with it the space for speaking comedically in its margins, is both impossible and inevitable. For the satanic reader, such a book of the cosmos is paradoxically exactly what cannot exist and precisely what must be burned and scattered in the furnace of Chaos as the ultimate expression of the most horrible heresy: the fact that anything is happening at all. This impulse, materialized in the initial scream of the opening track of Teutoburg Forest's *Anti-Subhuman Scum*, "Seeing God's Creation,

---

[14] "Nel suo profondo vidi che s'interna, / legato con amore in un volume, / ciò che per l'universo si squaderna: / sustanze e accidenti e lor costume / quasi conflati insieme, per tal modo / che ciò ch'i' dico è un semplice lume. / La forma universal di questo nodo / credo ch'i' vidi, perché più di largo, / dicendo questo, mi sento ch'i' godo" (Dante Alighieri, *The Divine Comedy*, ed. Charles S. Singleton [Princeton: Princeton University Press, 1973], *Paradiso* 33.85-93).

15

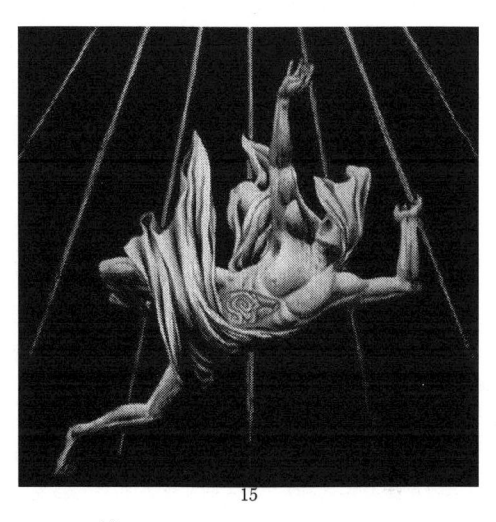

and Despising it,"¹⁶ is explicable as absolute refusal of the originary causality that the chain of being manifests, and more

---

¹⁵ Deathspell Omega, *Fas – Ite, Maledicti, in Ignem Aeternum* (Norma Evangelium Diaboli, 2005).

¹⁶ The absoluteness of the refusal signs itself in the double sense of the album title, at once indicating the stance of the album, its being against subhuman scum, and naming anti-subhumans, those who are against the subhuman, as scum. It dramatizes, in the mode of enmity, the negation of the negation, acknowledging that victory consists, not merely in the defeat of the enemy, but in the overcoming of the very terms of enmity and contest. This overcoming is not a secondary contest, not a second negation that follows after the first, but is contiguous with it in the pure holism of the *against* (Cf. Bataille's equation of the contestation of experience and the experience of contestation, cited above). *Anti-Subhuman Scum* is thus a statement of absolutizing elitism, a hate-exhausting psychic engine for transhumanation. The human (oneself-as-human) is overcome by

precisely, as hatred of the essential weakness or impotence of the absolute one who cannot not make others, the no-thing (*Ein Sof*) perfectly incapable of not creating many things. Plotinus explains:

> It is precisely because there is nothing within the One that all things are from it: in order that Being may be brought about, the source must be no Being but Being's generator, in what is to be thought as the primal act of generation. Seeking nothing, possessing nothing, lacking nothing, the One is perfect and, in our metaphor, has overflowed, and its exuberance has produced the new.[17]

As the angelic first link and primal mirror produced in this ecstatic emanation, Satan, second only to God, becomes archrival only, alonely, on the basis of being arch-other, the original subject of the most intimate and intolerable intersection between the absolute fact of God and something's being other than God.[18] In this the satanic principle is in essence the inversely maximal experience of the most minimal negation performed in the double ecstasy of creation, following Pseudo-Dionysius, who writes that "the very cause of the universe . . . is

---

including itself in that which it refuses as beneath itself. One hates God's creation to become a god—a trajectory spelled out in the album notes: "DO YOUR EYES SEE ALL THAT IS? / ARE WE MERE SLAVES BOUND BY EARTH? / OR GODS?"

[17] Plotinus, *Enneads*, trans. Stephen MacKenna (Burdett, NY: Larson, 1992), V.2.1.

[18] "Of all the mightes I haue made, moste nexte after me / I make the als master and merour of my mighte; / I beelde the here baynely in blys for to be, / I name the for Lucifer, als berar of lyghte" (*The York Plays*, ed. Richard Beadle [London: Edwin Arnold, 1982], lines 34-37).

also carried outside of himself . . . He is . . . enticed away from his transcendent dwelling place and comes to abide within all things, and he does so by virtue of his supernatural and ecstatic capacity to remain, nevertheless, within himself."[19] Hear this inverted in the voice of an *ego*: I, effect of the universe, am enclosed inside of myself, I am forced away from my transcendent dwelling place and come to abide outside of all things, and I do so by virtue of my supernatural and ecstatic capacity to remain, nevertheless, without myself.

[20]

Where, for whom, and to what end does this being speak? What is the discourse of the one who would evade this impossible enchainment, the extreme separation of the closest binding, who totally cannot tolerate cosmos as the place of

---

[19] Pseudo-Dionysius, *The Complete Works*, trans. Colm Luibheid and Paul Rorem (New York: Paulist Press, 1987), *Divine Names*, 4.13.

[20] Xasthur, *Xasthur* (Moribund, 2006).

being? Is there an anti-cosmic *logos* that is not "lost among babblers in a night in which we can only hate the appearance of light which comes from babbling"?[21] Is there a convivial, symposial anti-cosmosis, not merely a noise-making against, but a discursive noise that actually unmakes cosmos? Talking with his grandfather over the ear-filling pleasing sound of the celestial spheres [*qui complet aures meas tantus et tam dulcis sonus*], the younger Scipio learns of the twin telos of music and philosophy: "Gifted men, imitating this harmony on stringed instruments and in singing, have gained for themselves a return to this region, as have those who have devoted their exceptional abilities to a search for divine truths. The ears of mortals are filled with this sound, but they are unable to hear it."[22] My black mahapralaya inversely begins, unends my own beginning, by speaking while listening to what I am unable to hear within the dissonant metal that fills my mortal ears.[23]

---

[21] *Inner Experience*, xxxii.

[22] Macrobius, *Commentary on the Dream of Scipio*, 74.

[23] "Proceeding then to the falling tritone . . . I find more the feeling of shock that this man evokes in me [Cf. "What is this that stands before me? / Figure in black which points at me" (Black Sabbath, "Black Sabbath," *Black Sabbath*)]. But this feeling is connected with a kind of secret loosening up, as if I harbored the thought that I might use the evil in him to serve the evil hidden in me: I feel this possibility, this freedom in myself. What makes the tritone a *diabolus*, which is how J. S. Bach experienced it, is that it dissolves the threshold between inner world and outer world and permits the untransformed inner world to work into the outer world [Nietzsche's Zarathustra says: "For me—how could there be something outside me? There is no outside! But we forget this with all sounds; how lovely it is that we forget!" And the animals reply: "In every Instant being begins; round every Here rolls the ball. There. The middle is everywhere. Crooked is the

My cosmic dissolution begins, therefore, by ignoring both the anti-cosmic discourse of Gnostic occultism, which adorns itself in the drapery of Chaos like an enormous sigil-embroidered baby blanket, and the anti-discourse world of consumerist metal fandom. I ignore these, remain consciously and willfully stupid towards them, in favor of their simple, practical synthesis: the dialectical pleasure of hearing and thinking black metal as itself an occult experience of the cosmic abyss.[24] In other words, I embrace as axiomatic the effective fact

---

path of eternity" (*Thus Spoke Zarathustra*, trans. Adrian Del Caro [Cambridge: Cambridge University Press, 2006], 'The Convalescent', 175)]. . . . The impulse of my untempered inner nature to realize itself in the outer world arrogantly and without undergoing transformation is one side of the devil, the Luciferic side. The other side is in the tendency of the realities of the outer world to pour untransformed into my inner world where they can 'pulverize' (Rudolf Steiner's expression) my soul, working deeply into the anxieties and compulsions of my subconscious where they establish themselves as the sole ruler–this is the Satanic ('Ahrimanic') side. Naturally, today we can also begin to sense dimly in the tritone how two worlds that are diametrically opposed as regards time, the inner world and the outer world, resolve themselves into a unity when they are experienced from the aspect of eternity–and this is the truly atonal experience of the triton which the 20th century has begun to find" (Heiner Ruland, *Expanding Tonal Awareness: A Musical Exploration of the Evolution of Consciousness Guided by the Monochord*, trans. John F. Logan [Sussex: Rudolf Steiner Press, 1992], 96).

[24] "Spiritual experience involves more than can be grasped by mere intellect. This is often emphasised by calling it a mystical experience. Mysticism is often regarded as something anti-intellectual, obscure and confused, or impractical and unconnected with experience. In fact, true mysticism is none of these. *There is nothing irrational in true mysticism when it is, as it should be, a vision of Reality. It is a form of perception which is*

that black metal is only what has already stripped me of banal belonging to the universe as the place of being, restored to appearance the primal fact that her existence and mine are coeval, that we go way back—a sonic "ecstatic, breathless, *experience* . . . [that] opens a bit more every time the horizon of God (the wound); extends a bit more the limits of the heart, the limits of being."[25] Not for the sake of knowing true black metal from false, but for being truthful about it. The anti-cosmic structure of such metallic factical blackening of experience,

26

---

absolutely unclouded, and so practical that it can be lived every moment of life and expressed in everyday duties" (Meher Baba, *Discourses*, I.20). "Il y a un autre monde mais il est dans celui-ci" (Paul Éluard).

[25] Georges Bataille, *Inner Experience*, 104.
[26] Arckanum, *The 11th Year Anniversary Album* (Carnal, 2004). "Within the numerological context 0 is the symbol of the womb of the zeroth dimensional Chaos, while 1 stands for the contracting (coagula)

and forming/ordering impulse of the cosmic creation/creator. All numbers from 1-10 stand for the different stages of causal creation and emanation, which culminate in the number 10 that stands for cosmic completion. 10 also stands for law, order, manifestation of form, restriction, the closed circle that within itself has captured the fallen Flames of Chaos, the ego/'I' and the repression of the Acausal Self. Eleven, which is the number of Anti-Cosmic Chaos, symbolizes therefore that which steps over and goes beyond the cosmic 10. Eleven stands for lawlessness, freedom, formlessness and the breaking of the closed circle. Eleven is the gate to the primeval Chaos and the road through which the essence can transcend the restrictions of forms. Therefore, eleven also symbolizes the completion of Anti-Cosmic Evolution and the realization of hidden, dark and Acausal potential. The Eleven Angled Sigil (the sigil of Azerate and the Temple of the Black Light) is therefore a sigilic manifestation of Gnosis that with its eleven angles can open the Dark Gate (Black Hole) to Acausal freedom beyond the limitations of cosmic law and existence" (<http://www.templeoftheblacklight.net/library/chaosophy/chaosophy.html>). "The number eleven as it exceeds the number ten, which is the number of the commandements [commandments], so it fals short of the number twelve, which is of grace and perfection, therefore it is called the number of sins, and the penitent. Hence in the tabernacle there were commanded to be made eleven Coats of hair which is the habit of those that are penitent, and lament for their sins, whence this number hath no Communion with Divine or Celestiall things, nor any attraction, or scale tending to things above: neither hath it any reward; but yet sometimes it receives a gratuitous favor from God, as he which was called the eleventh hour to the vineyard of the Lord, received the same reward as those who had born the burden, and heat of the day" (Heinrich Cornelius Agrippa, *Occult Philosophy*, 2.14). "In each cycle of time, which ranges from 700 to 1400 years, there are eleven ages of 65 to 125 years each. From the beginning to the end of each cycle, there are altogether 55 Perfect Masters and that means each age has only five (5) Perfect Masters. In the last, the eleventh age of each cycle, the which makes the whole moment of life immediately fulfill Quentin Meillassoux's definition of facticity as the "narrow passage through which thought is able to exit from itself . . . [and] we are able to make our way towards the absolute,"[27] is perfectly explicit in Shamaatae of Arckanum's cosmos-collapsing self-definitions: "I am a living and revolving cosmos of Kaos. I can't stay as one and in one way;" "Chaos theory is a theory

---

Avatar (Saheb-e-Zaman) is also present. Besides the 55 Perfect Masters and the *Avatar* there are also 56 *Majzoobs-e-Kamil* in each cycle. These *Majzoobs*, who experience the state of *fana-fillah*, are the 'sleeping' or 'inactive' partners in the conduct of the divine sport (*lila*) of Creation" (Meher Baba, *God Speaks*, p. 254 [2+5+4=11]). "Eleven is the mystic number throughout Carnival" (Godfrey Fey, "Carnival in the Rhineland," *Folklore* 71 (1960): 48). *Cyclonopedia* begins with eleven: "11 March 2004" (Reza Negarestani, *Cyclonopedia* [Melbourne: re.press, 2008], 9); note that the date also resolves to eleven (1+1+3+2+0+0+4=11). In short, eleven is the enumeration of that which is above number: "Ten and not eleven [sefiroth]: this is to exclude from the enumeration that hidden thing that stands at the beginning of *kether*. For if we behold an end [of *kether*] at the beginning of the paths of *hokhmah*, one might think that *kether* too has a beginning. Hence that which is above it is a hidden thing beyond all thought and speech, and which does not enter into any enumeration" (Nahmanides's commentary on Yesirah 1:4, cited from Gershom Scholem, *Origins of the Kabbalah*, ed. R. J. Zwi Werblowsky, trans. Allan Arkush [Princeton: Princeton University Press, 1987], 433).

[27] Quentin Meillassoux, *After Finitude: An Essay on the Necessity of Contingency*, trans. Ray Brassier (London: Continuum, 2008), 63. Cf. "Not *how* the world is, is the mystical, but *that* it is" (Ludwig Wittgenstein, *Tractatus Logico-Philosophicus*, tr. C.K. Ogden [Mineola, NY: Dover Publications, 1998], 6.44).

that structures my way of living, I am chaos theory in flesh. . . . I am my own influence."[28]

That this black metal shaman understands himself not only as Chaos personified but as a self-originating incarnation of its *theory*, "theory in flesh," opens and outdeepens the significance of the premature anti-discursive commentary on this symposium which, in inimical collusion with my own quixotic nigredic purposes, summons the intersecting problems of anti-cosmic discourse and the theoretical occult, *the space of relation between what cannot be spoken and the speech that destroys*. Someone called The Scapegoat, sacrificing the law to maintain it, declares that "the first rule of black metal is that YOU DO NOT FUCKING TALK ABOUT BLACK METAL."[29] Cum Crémed Guts, who lists his location as "cosmic womb of abyss" and so suggests his own primordial identity with the inseminated viscera of the *mater omnium*, observes: "i thought one puts occult into his black metal, not the other way around."[30] And Extra Cheese Head trollishly quips discourse (as a form of irrelevant fantasy, inauthentic affect, and social weakness) in a way that indicates the special generic authority of black metal as a grottophilic space of absolute refusal: "yep I think Fenriz and the likes would laugh their asses off if they saw this bunch of D&D playing, pseudo-misanthropics huddling together and attempting to scholarize something as blatantly anti-everything as black metal."[31] These comments sonically perpetuate the stagnancy of

---

[28] <http://www.chroniclesofchaos.com/articles/chats/1-123_arckanum.aspx>, <http://www.bloodchamber.de/interview/a/5/>, respectively.

[29] <http://www.foreverdoomed.com/forums/>.

[30] <http://www.fmp666.com/forum/>.

[31] <http://decibelmagazine.com/forum/>.

a separative and self-preserving vision, one that blindly holds the unseeable in collective eclipse as the only way of looking at it.

I see here, in the darkness of my own self-projection, a ridiculous doubleness. On the one hand: cultic love of an authentic occult, the experience of subjectively accessed realities whose theory, unlike that of sciences which concern commonly observable and manipulable phenomena, "can in no way approximate direct knowledge in import and significance."[32] On the other hand: the hopeless failure of the solely theoretical occultist who, because "occult realities are bound to remain for them more or less in the same category as descriptions of unseen lands or works of imagination," perversely falls to accusing others of ignorance as the (ego's) last remaining option or investment in the hermetic mode of instruction: teaching

---

[32] Meher Baba, *Discourses*, II.102.

those who already know.[33] This vulgar policing of the space of authentic experience, which proceeds by holding forever closed the meeting place of theory and practice, science and art, philosophy and poetry, shutting them up in the minimally present and maximally interviewable person of the master to whom alone is accorded the privilege of a theoretical gnosis, defines a position fatally prone to drawing the wrong conclusion from Arckanum's body, namely: that there can be no black metal theory because black metal is flesh. Impossibilizing black metal discourse in the paradoxical mode of a tiny, pathetic illumination that might expose its primal night as a cave-dweller's fantasy, such anxious refusal of the blackening, darkness-deepening potentiality of thought betrays faithlessness

---

[33] For example: "Since the TOTBL [Temple of the Black Light] has reached is predetermined number of fully initiated brothers and sisters, membership is closed, but it is still our duty to reach out and offer guidance to the very few who bear within them the Black Flames of the acosmic Spirit. So while we do not offer initiation into the Inner Sanctum at this time, we still offer relevant parts of the Chaosophic teachings that we believe can lead the elect of our Gods to the illumination of the Black Light. The texts presented on this website have as their purpose to test the readers, confuse the feeble-minded majority, and guide the very few of spiritual work to other, more hidden points of ingress into the very heart of the Current 218. A secondary motive for the outside manifestation of the Anti-Cosmic Tradition is to counteract the essenceless and materialistic filth that is spread in the name of Satan and Satanism. By presenting a spiritual and yet harshly antinomian form of Gnostic Luciferianism, we hope to contribute to the establishment of visible alternatives to the vulgarism preached by atheistic con men. *Incipit Chaos!*" (<http://www.templeoftheblacklight.net/main.html>).

in the awesome reality of the abyss, which, whatever anyone names it, is absolutely divine.[34]

![Chao Ab Ordo album cover]

These are the torments of each, of all who wrestle in collective solitude with the terrifying discontinuous continuities and continuous discontinuities between the reality of what is

---

[34] *Id est*, facticity is God. "The Disciple said to his Master: Sir, How may I come to the supersensual Life, so that I may see God, and may hear God speak? The Master answered and said: Son, when thou canst throw thyself into THAT, where no creature dwelleth, though it be but for a moment, then thou hearest what God speaketh. *Disciple*: Is that where no creature dwelleth near at hand; or is it afar off? *Master*: It is in thee. And if thou canst, my Son, for a while but cease from all thy thinking and willing, then thou shalt hear the unspeakable words of God" (Jacob Boehme, *Of the Supersensual Life* [Cambridge: James Clarke, 1969], 227). "Thou art That" (*Chandogya Upanisad*, VI.8.7).

[35] Teutoburg Forest, *Chao Ab Ordo* (2008).

loved and the image of thought. And this pain points the way (backwards or forwards?) into the superior, more pleasurable suffering wherein the noble lover, the immoderate cogitator of Andreas Capellanus's *De Amore*, the one who loves thinking about the loved one (black metal), who knows that "loving is also necessarily a speculation . . . an essentially phantasmatic process, involving both imagination and memory in an assiduous, tormented circling around an image painted or reflected in the deepest self," this one both knows full well the reality of the thought-image he loses himself in and wholly enjoys its actualization of the original dark out of which it and his own being strangely appear:

> For then my thoughts, far from where I abide,
> Intend a zealous pilgrimage to thee,
> And keep my drooping eyelids open wide,
> Looking on darkness which the blind do see.
> Save that my soul's imaginary sight
> Presents thy shadow to my sightless view,
> Which like a jewel hung in ghastly night,
> Makes black night beauteous, and her old face new.[36]

Here we see the lovely, speculative hideous gnosis of an essentially citational erotic consciousness, the unnamable entity who, sitting in the medieval chained library of the body, practices loving things in the intellectual mirror of his ownmost cosmic abyss. Such a one not only passes the highest, Dantean test of occult authenticity, proving knowledge of hidden realities

---

[36] William Shakespeare, *Sonnets*, edited with analytic commentary by Stephen Booth (New Haven: Yale University Press, 1977), 27.5-12.

[image: Mütiilation, *Black Millenium (Grimly Reborn)* album cover]

37

by the joy of speaking about them,[38] but flies with Walter Benjamin's ungenerated androgynous angelic self, Agesilaus Santander, kabbalistically interpreted by his scholarly friend Gershom Scholem as an anagram of *The Angel Satan* (*Der Angelus*

---

[37] Mütiilation, *Black Millenium (Grimly Reborn)* (Drakkar, 2001).

[38] On the question of authenticating occult experience, Meher Baba writes: "occult experiences often bear unmistakeable credentials for their own claim to validity, and even when any such credentials are not evident they compel due respect and attention because of the unusual significance, bliss, peace and directive value with which they are surcharged. . . . ordinary hallucinations and delusions do not bring extraordinary bliss or peace to the person who experiences them. The bliss and peace which are attendant upon real occult experiences are a fairly reliable criterion by which to distinguish them as genuine" (*Discourses*, II.88-9).

Satanas).[39] This angel, whose ideal is a book that "would eliminate all commentary and consist in nothing but quotations," teaches the shocking citational discourse of living tradition that "does not aim to perpetuate and repeat the past but to lead it to its decline in a context in which past and present, content of transmission and act of transmission, what is unique and what is repeatable, are wholly identified."[40] In other words, the happy, Satanic *catena*, whose dissonant rattle black metal already is, destroys cosmos by means of its own chain of

---

[39] On Agesilaus Santander, see Steven M. Wasserstrom, *Religion After Religion: Gershom Scholem, Mircea Eliade, and Henry Corbin at Eranos* (Princeton: Princeton University Press, 1999), 206ff.

[40] Giorgio Agamben, "Walter Benjamin and the Demonic: Happiness and Historical Redemption," in *Potentialities: Collected Essays in Philosophy*, trans. Daniel Heller-Roazen (Stanford: Stanford University Press, 1999), 153. Walter Benjamin"s "ideal was a book that would eliminate all commentary and consist in nothing but quotations" (Françoise Meltzer, "Acedia and Melancholia," in *Walter Benjamin and the Demands of History*, ed. Michael P. Steinberg [Ithaca: Cornell University Press, 1996], 162). Why? Because "in citation old and new are brought into simultaneity" (Eva Geulen, "Counterplay: Benjamin," chapter 4 of *The End of Art: Readings in a Rumour After Hegel*, trans. James McFarland [Stanford: Stanford University Press, 2006], 87): "To the traditionalizing effects of commentary, Benjamin . . . opposes the citation as *shock*, which shatters the continuum and which does not resolve itself in any solution of continuity; and, on the other hand, the citation as *montage* . . . in which the fragments come into connection in order to form a constellation intelligible to the present" (Phillipe Simay, "Tradition as Injunction: Benjamin and the Critique of Historicisms," in *Walter Benjamin and History*, ed. Andrew Benjamin [London: Continuum, 2005], 147).

being,[41] realizing the temporal present of the word as the original whim from beyond,[42] named by Reza Negarestani as

---

[41] The sonic *how* of this destruction operates via the three forms of black noise that attach to all aesthetic objects: "To summarize, we have a real intention whose core is inhabited by a real me and a sensual pine tree. In addition, there is also a withdrawn real tree (or something that we mistake for one) lying outside the intention, but able to affect it along avenues still unknown. Finally, the sensual tree never appears in the form of a naked essence, but is always encrusted with various sorts of noise. Elsewhere I have called it 'black noise', to emphasize that it is highly structured, not the sort of formless chaos suggested by the 'white noise' of television and radio. Black noise initially seems to come in three varieties. First, the sensual tree has pivotal or essential qualities that must always belong to it under penalty of the intentional agent no longer considering it the same thing. Second, the tree has accidental features shimmering along its surface from moment to moment, not affecting our identification of it as one and the same. Finally, the pine tree stands in relation to countless peripheral objects that inhabit the same intention (neighboring trees, mountains, deer, rabbits, clouds of mist)" (Graham Harman, "On Vicarious Causation," *Collapse II* (2007): 182-3). These three forms of black noise correspond to the triune genero-psychic dimensions through which black metal begets itself in procession. 1) Essential qualities belonging to entities under pain of no longer thinking it the same: such quality is the domain of Occult Black Metal, which is devoted to the hidden (esoteric, orthodox, kabbalistic, apophatic etc.), to accessing what lies outside the intention but still affects it via *avenues unknown*. 2) Accidental features shimmering along the surface from moment to moment: such quality is the domain of Profane Black Metal (hedonist, punk, heedless), which is about exposing and mocking life as pure contentless appearance. 3) Standing in relation to countless peripheral objects: such quality belongs to the thrown contextual space of Melancholic (black-biled) Black Metal, which is concerned with expressing the deepest and self-dissolving relations between things, the

"*Incognitum Hactenus*—not known yet or nameless and without origin until now . . . In *Incognitum Hactenus*, you never know the pattern of emergence. Anything can happen for some weird reason; yet also, without any reason, nothing at all can happen."[43]

You too will come to proclaim *it's* ultimate presence.

---

abyssic proximities between and within entities, intimate links to the non-relatable, the fact that one is, and so on. Via dissonant resonances within and among these three phenomenal nodes, black metal vibrationally unhinges the order of things, tritonely crushes all holy trinities, annihilates every binding of the chain of being.

[42] "The unitarian Beyond is an indivisible and indescribable infinity. *It seeks to know itself.* It is of no use to ask why it does so. To attempt to give a reason for this is to be involved in further questions and thus to start an unending chain of reasons and so on *ad infinitum*. The plain truth about this initial urge to know itself is best called a whim (*Lahar*). A whim is not a whim if it can be explained or rationalized. And just as no one may usefully ask why it arises, so no one may ask when it arises. 'When' implies a time series with past, present and future. All these are absent in the eternal Beyond. So let us call this initial urge to know a 'whim.' You may call this an explanation if you like or you may call it an affirmation of its inherent inexplicability. The initial whim is completely independent of reason, intellect or imagination, all of which are by-products of this whim. . . . This whim of the Infinte is in a way comparable to an infinite question, calling forth an infinite answer" (Meher Baba, "The Whim from Beyond," *Beams*, 8-9).

[43] Reza Negarestani, *Cyclonopedia: Complicity with Anonymous Materials* (Melbourne: re.press, 2008), 49.

[44] Spiralling anomaly seen in the pre-dawn Norwegian sky three days before Hideous Gnosis.

PERPETUE PUTESCO – PERPETUALLY I PUTREFY
Joseph Russo

> Change through subtraction, or the mobilization of extensive and intensive vectors in regard to each other, is the very Idea of decay.
> —Reza Negarestani

> And Darkness and Decay and the Red Death held illimitable dominion over all.
> —Edgar Allan Poe

This exploration attempts to engage the obsessions of black metal with the utility of decay as a twofold event. Here is an attempt to map out the connections between the so-called themes of decay with the actuality of the decay of sound, which has emerged, largely over the past decade, in various exploratory subgenres of black metal. What is of the highest interest to me are the levels of disconnection between these two forms of expressing decay, what I refer to as moments of rupture. A third form of decay will be exposed in the process of examining the first two, and these are the moments of rupture that plague any expression. The third form of decay is a result of various human interests, insinuating themselves before that un-harnessed void of dark expressions, thus sullying the so-called singularity of said expressions. In short, the immediacy of the expression is compromised variously by, among other things: the dogged insistence of normativity upon what is rightfully aberrant, by the presupposition of various political agendas, and by the demands of an industry whose most effective means of profit requires the formulaic homogenizing of the genre.

These assertions would seem to suggest that black metal largely fails to deliver its promises of dark epiphanies; however, these observations are only to understand black metal as being susceptible to the same forces of stabilization and homogenization that accompany all processes of transaction between creator and devotee. Thus, not only is all music that is sold to the public privy to these stultifying forces that allow only for potential (in the case of black metal, this is the underlying potential of the body and mind's total immersion in an immeasurable void) transactions, but it also seems to be true that black metal is one of the forms of expression that in some sense laments, if not fully combats this stagnating potentiality between the musician and his song, between the song and its listeners, between the body and mind, and between the void and its various harnesses. After all, what is truly revelatory to many devoted listeners of any given genre emerges from the moments of possible divergence from these predetermined regulations of sound. That is, the moments when an artist somehow vaults the pool of normalcy, even for a moment, to deliver a singular something (even if it is only a singular something in the ears of a handful of rabid devotees) that proves the instability, moreover the perpetual decay of any given system.

The primary level of decay conveyed in black metal concerns the predisposition toward matters of the human body's decomposition. A recurring scenario involves the ritualistic debasement of the decomposing corpse at the hands of the living, in what can often be understood as a de-sanctifying ritual that rids the rotting corpse of its illusory spiritual wholeness. In a sense, this restores what in black metal is considered the primal, or pre-Christian integrity of the body as a perpetually rotting vessel, a body wrapped in falsehood by the bankrupt morality of religious rituals, such as Catholic Anointing or Unction of the Sick, where the dying body's ever-distrustful soul is hurriedly given back to itself by the priest as having been something other than only a body. In so doing, metal consciously repositions the voyage of the human body through its physiological moments of rupture, such that the phrase: "From the moment we are born, we are dying," takes on a more threatening implication, perhaps being re-worded as: "From the moment we are composed of matter, we are rotting." I feel that this moment is where much metal dwells, in this liminal death-space. The rotting is revealed as the essence which has structured the illusions of the life itself, as in the lyrics from Celestia's "The Seeds of Negation" (from the album *Frigidiia Apotheosia: Abstinencia*, Paragon/Apparitia 2008): "So, I will wait, sit on my throne, gazing at the sky, in search of answers and time will fade out, slowly over my corpse. Day after day, I rot, expecting light that will bless me for the rest of eternity. I will tend to forget the taste of all the Seeds I had to taste . . ." In the same removal of the body from the blind procession of the sacraments, the mind of the speaker simultaneously conceives of its rotting physiology, undergoing a reconfiguration of its own; that is, the physical aspect of the brain's decomposition finds a hostile counterpart in the putrefaction of its immaterial projections: its thoughts or dreams.

Second, it can certainly be said that black metal, in its varying and perpetually evolving states, employs a literal decomposition and decay of its own presence; that is, the sound of the metal itself is, in a sense, rotting away before our very ears. This aesthetic, which cannot merely be reduced to the labeling of the sound as "lo-fi" (because in many cases, as with Xasthur, the sound often undertakes a decaying progression from clarity and fullness to confusion and disparity), finds many forms in the tradition of black metal. A general rejection of metal's adherence to pristinely recorded music permeated the sound of many progenitors of the genre's sound (Darkthrone, Burzum) from the very beginning of their recorded output. However, in the case of more contemporary recordings, such as those of Xasthur or Wold, this rejection of clarity is taken to its utmost conceptual level. Beyond merely producing a record that sounds grimy, faraway, muddled, etc, these artists create a presence that is wholly separate from the music. That is, the decay of the sound is so prevalent that it merits a separate analysis by the listener. If we are to understand these dual drives of rot (the obsession with rot and the aural presence of rot) as necessitating each other's existences, then the music of Xasthur can be said to not only obsess over rot, but to rot itself, perpetually reminding, or resetting the potential of an exponentially sped up deterioration within the mind of the listener.

On the other hand, as is often the case in much death metal, there is the concept of decay as being bound up in the natural, and therefore being part of that composite organism called the human body, the declared enemy of the genre. The body, along with its faculties of natural decay, must be disrupted by the immediacy of dismemberment, the rupturing of all spaces of the human body into one reconfigured, open space. A hollow corpse, or a corpse without borders, is necessary for the satiation of these anti-conceptual urges. It destroys the possibility of reflection; the corpse is no longer a corpse, it can no longer be looked upon as a corpse, nor can it look upon itself with any recognition. In fact, it could be said that for much death metal whose chief preoccupation lays in gore-mongering, that the body itself is a host of speculative pathways, a possibility zone of great threat. The process of auto-deterioration is often challenged as a kind of turgid, slow debasement of the flesh; natural deterioration offers a kind of challenge to the body's owner to advance decay. It is only after disfigurement and debasement of the corpse take place that necrophilic urges can emerge, in which the corpse is wallowed in, raped, or sodomized in a ritual of great satisfaction, as in Decay's song, "Copulation With the Gutted Corpse": "Hollow corpse, vile swarming, overwhelming, internal organs consumed, infested cavities, decayed remnants, sickness of the flesh, necroticism, perverse cannibalism, molesting the dead . . . Fucked. Morbid carnage on the dead flesh, eating from the rotting orifice" (Gutting 2001). The vile pleasure-epiphany that is encapsulated within the expression of the song, then, seems to require a deep confusion of the physical essence of beings, so that what is being interacted with must reside in a state of physiological bewilderment in order for the speaker to so poetically transcribe his gratification.

Oppositely, as in what I feel Xasthur is doing, a good deal of the thematic and aural expressions give precedence to decay not of the body, as it were, but of the mind. Much black metal attempts to provide a hammer, both metaphysical and aural, that can rid the flesh of its illusory snares. Obviously, the recurring polarity lies between God and the Devil, or more accurately, between God and His Absence. Indeed, Xasthur's void-worlds, such as the flooded abysmal depths, seem to engulf this preoccupation with the God-rituals and trinkets of Catholic Mass that a lot of artists in the genre have dwelt upon with a monomaniacal insistence. Dominic Fox of Poetix blog finds this preoccupation rather questionable, when he inquires: "Does not such studious blasphemy betray a perverse attachment to its object?" In other words, a great deal of anti-Christian black metal maintains a knowledge of such objects that are lost to the now predominant rabble of evangelical Christians, whose masses often take place in fluorescent-lit recreation centers and whose priests often wear sweatsuits. After all, how can the relation of the apse to the nave be considered as a demon's phallus, or the ciborium be defecated in, when these very objects have been rendered obsolete, the frivolity of their ornate natures sacrificed in favor of a more easily accessible road to God? This is the God whose kingdom only demands that one become "born again" upon entry, in a ludicrous pantomime of that other great fallacy of sacraments: baptism. In what is perhaps a pre-emptive strike against the plasticized delegation whose moments of rapture are blatantly manufactured,[1] Xasthur's abysmal depths bear little resemblance to any common notion of the Inferno. The expressions of suffering entailed within the song are so gruesome precisely because the body is not suffering; it is not doing anything, as such. In fact, the ability of being is itself suspended: there is no possibility in the void-world for quantifiable suffering and, therefore, not only is the suffering endless, it is not locatable. The subject of the song is himself also rendered undetectable, detailing his role

---

[1] For a perfect example of this floundering in the absence of any heightened state, see the "speaking in tongues" scene of the 2006 documentary film Jesus Camp, in which not only is a specific time designated for the *entire* parish's partaking in glossolalia, but also the entire group force themselves into paroxysms of fake mumbling and chattering *when they are prompted to do so*, and can therefore cease responding to the throes of their "possession" just as swiftly.

both as torturer and tortured, yet speculating upon the futility of both positions with the lyrics: "Will there even be a word known as death anymore, when left is nothing to kill?" ("Abysmal Depths Are Flooded", from the album *Telepathic With The Deceased*, 2004) Xasthur elsewhere addresses urges the body/mind schism to destroy the human presence behind its conception; this destruction is a possible pathway into Xasthur's void-worlds, for it is the place where the liminal state is most fully realized. The abysmal depths of Xasthur are a-temporal, they somehow stagnate from a location outside of normative measurements of time, and the mourning in blackness is not merely born out of a contempt for God and love for Satan, but for the contempt of that idea of a mere duality, so absurdly simple in its morality, structuring the very framework of our tortured existences.

Xasthur offers to eternally unclasp those falsehoods of vitalism in "Murdered Echoes Of The Mind." This is where material decay becomes incidental, and where the concept of self proliferates endlessly in all of its possible decayed states. This ruinous nullification finds its ancestry in, among other things, Poe's character M. Valdemar, whose body lies, for some time, suspended in the liminal state. When the mesmerist who has originally captivated the dying Valdemar finally releases him from his wretched stasis, the body putrefies instantly: "his whole frame at once—within the space of a single minute, or even less, shrunk—crumbled—absolutely rotted away beneath my hands. Upon the bed, before that whole company, there lay a nearly liquid mass of loathsome—of detestable putridity" ("The Facts In The Case Of M. Valdemar," Poe 109). Perhaps this is the spawning ground of Xasthur's urge to decay, emerging from the possibility of eradicating, or degrading, the mind. The body, as such, needs not be assaulted in order to achieve rupture, for it has always only rotted; only the false concepts associated with the fertile arc of a godly life, imposed upon the body, ever confused this. This illusion having been eradicated, the body is able to rid itself of the conceptual structures that separated it from its perpetual deterioration. For M.Valdemar, this meant instant putrefaction; for the captivated of Xasthur's ritual, it suggests a gateway into the void, in which the void is not a final resting-place or eternal place of suffering within a spiritual vacuum, but the place where the revelatory, infinite states of rot, are cyclically re-experienced. It is the repetition that, as in Robin Mackay's comment on Negarestani on decay, "looks directly into the black pit" (Mackay 1). The mind, caught in a pre-birthing/post-mortem loop, a kind of repeated intra-uterine fetal demise, teeters cruelly on the verge of birth and death.

Mackay begins to answer the question of what is specifically revelatory within the entrapment of infinite decay; what does gazing into the black pit reveal? This is perhaps most fruitfully explored through Negarestani's statement: ". . . that the decay of a being traverses the cosmology of other beings" (Mackay 3). This seems to insist that the nature of decay complexifies our understanding and observation of not only Aristotelian, taxonomically-based difference, but muddles the stratifications of difference on a larger, conceptual level. That is, when does one being begin to differ from another being, and more specifically: if in the process of decay, the decaying being becomes other beings, then there is also the larger implication that decay: "reconfigures nature as an infinite reservoir for anomalous recombinations" (2). If it is indeed the cosmology of other beings that is being traversed, as Negarestani insists, then decay, as a conceptual tool, would be a possible route for a being attempting to evade the false singularity of its consciousness, to rot univocally in a Deleuzean sense; that is, to rot as perpetual Difference.[2]

This concept of decay being a vessel for the consistent flux of forms, a pathway through which beings experience various, momentary incarnations, is perhaps most graphically accentuated by another exploration of Negarestani's, in which he discusses the nigredo. As described in the eighth book of Aeneid, there was a form of torture used by the Etruscans in which: "A living man or woman was tied to a rotting corpse, face to face, mouth to mouth, limb to limb, with an obsessive exactitude in which each part of the body corresponded with its matching putrefying counterpart. Shackled to their rotting double, the man or woman was left to decay" (Negarestani 131). Eventually, the body of the victim began to blacken as the external decay manifested. However, as the Etruscans had it, this was merely the surfacing of an already occurring and perpetual decay, located within the body. The blackening proffered by the corpse bride onto its host, then, is not so much

---

[2] For instance, Mackay mentions Henry of Hesse (1325-1397), a fourteenth century scholar whose work in early scientific observation refuted Aristotelian notions of identification, replacing the concepts of taxonomy with a method of quantification that measures the "latitude," or range, of various intensities such as heat, cold, dryness, and wetness upon the physical integrity of the subject's body. The example is given that, under Hesse's latitude of forms, a draft horse would be considered in the same zoological group or zone as an ox, rather than with other kinds of horses that are used for different purposes, such as racehorses. This is because the draft horse is susceptible to a similar range of latitudes that are more closely related to the experience of oxen. In what is normatively considered outlandish hypothesizing, Hesse asserted that in its process of decay, a dog could *become*, as it were, a fox.

an infestation as a revelatory catalyst. This mirrors the strategy of black metal, which, rather than enacting that which is inevitable upon the body, strips away the illusions that the body shackles itself within, propelling it toward the multiplicity of being. The great luxury of the genre is, of course, the ability of the listener to unbind himself from the corpse bride, and return to Xbox360 in the basement of his parent's suburban home.

This is true of any work that can be switched off, of course, but perhaps takes on a more absurd significance in the case of black metal. This is largely due to the utter seriousness and devotion that most followers of the genre treat the material, often pledging a commitment to black metal that reaches far beyond mere appreciation. The simultaneous demands of a workaday American life upon these devotees is often absurdly juxtaposed,[3] having struck my pre-teen mind as both a beautifully poetic struggle, and often a quixotic, self-righteous frivolity. As it stands, black metal is one of those specialized genres of music that demands this kind of reverence, not unlike other exceedingly specified subgenres. Even gaining the ability to differentiate between the nuanced variations of the subgenre takes a devotion to the details and precision of sound that is altogether uncommon (and growing more uncommon) in the average listener. The record collection of the black metal devotee may specify hundreds or thousands of instances of decay, pestilence, and the encumbering body's dissolution. Therefore, this obsessively devotional stance in black metal makes its devotee into a decay archivist, plumbing the great

---

[3] For a beautiful simultaneous satire/homage of the life of the suburban black metaller, see the gorgeous black metal montage of Harmony Korine's 1999 film *Gummo*.

black mass of rot for further decaying processes with which to unshackle the self from its illusory conceptions.

WORKS CITED

Celestia. "The Seeds Of Negation" – from the LP *Frigidiis Apotheosia: Abstinencia Genesiis*, Paragon Records, Apparitia Recordings (US and French Releases) 2008.

Decay. "Copulation With The Gutted Corpse" – from the demo CD non-label release Gutting (2001).

Fox, Dominic. "Paint The Devil On The Wall." Poetix blog. February 12th, 2007 entry.

Mackay, Robin. "On Reza Negarestani's *Undercover Softness* (Philosophical and Aesthetic Tangents)."

Negarestani, Reza. "The Corpse Bride: Thinking with Nigredo." *Collapse* IV (2009): 129-60.

Poe, Edgar Allen. *Tales Of Mystery & Imagination*. "The Facts In The Case of M. Valdemar". The Franklin Mystery Library, 1987.

Xasthur. "Abysmal Depths Are Flooded" & "Murdered Echoes Of The Mind" - From the LP *Telepathic With The Deceased*, Moribund Records (US CD Release), From Beyond Productions, (Netherlands 2 x LP version) 2004.

'*REMAIN TRUE TO THE EARTH!*': REMARKS ON THE POLITICS OF BLACK METAL
Benjamin Noys

Der Feind is unsre eigene Frage als Gestalt.

—Carl Schmitt

If we were to define a degree zero of Black Metal politics then it would be an unstable amalgam of Stirnerite egoism and Nietzschean aristocratism: a radical anti-humanist individualism implacably hostile to all the ideological 'spooks' of the present social order, committed to creating an 'aristocracy of the future' (Nietzsche 464), and auto-engendering a 'creative nothing' (Stirner 6). The instability lies in the coupling of a disabused hostility to liberal-capitalist ideologemes with a Nietzschean 'grand politics' of natural degrees and ranks. More precisely it lies in the retention of certain radicalised 'spooks' – notably nation, race, historical tradition or counter-tradition, and war – that perform the dual function of disrupting the limits of acceptable discourse within modern liberal democracies and *grounding* the abyssal draining of all ideological contents. Of course these are often 'spooks' associated with the extreme right, Nazism, fascism, and ultra-nationalism. Whereas Stirnerite individualism might be regarded as anarchist, or at best indifferent to politics, this racial-national metaphysics is often, although not always of course, deployed to re-territorialise and establish a 'grand politics'.

It can be argued that it is perfectly possible to detach such a politics, which often seems at best secondary or contingent, from Black Metal as a musical practice. A contrast can be drawn between a musical radicalism that is betrayed or constrained by these 'remnants' of theo-politics. In this way the critic from the left can safely handle and enjoy Black Metal and proclaim their sophistication by condescending to the naiveté of such adolescent political posturing which 'unfortunately' marks an otherwise admirably radical aesthetic. It is even possible that this distancing could permit a disavowed *enjoyment* of the radically politically-incorrect posturing of certain forms of Black Metal. We can imagine a more sophisticated Deleuzoguattarian version of this argument: the deterritorialising or dematerialising effect of Black Metal *qua* music requires a reterritorialising grounding *qua* politics, but only to produce a necessary site of radicalised intensification; after all, the nomad performs their deterritorialisation by staying in place.

The implication of this argument is that the various territorialised 'spooks' that haunt Black Metal are mere thresholds or sedimentations that, despite its own proclaimed territoriality, Black Metal works over, exceeds, and puts in flight. Evan Calder Williams has given this type of argument a more Marxist inflection: 'the lesson to be drawn from black metal is the way in which its concrete sonic expression dismantles its spoken ideology.' (Misanthropy) In this case the clashing and disruptive 'avant-garde' elements of Black Metal's musical praxis bear witness to the inner decay of the contemporary bourgeois order and, at the same time, deterritorialise its own reactive re-territorialisation of such decay onto a new order of 'purity'. Black Metal is presented as auto-deconstructive, immanently acepahlic, and, in line with the self-presentation of many Black Metal artists, deliberately self-parodic. Contrary to its own subjective political presentation,

Black Metal objectively, in its aesthetic, forms a utopian and immanent critique of the misery of neo-liberal capitalism.

Despite the temptations of such claims they refuse to take seriously the kind of coherence between aesthetics and politics argued for from *within* Black Metal. Instead of a splitting or contradiction between de-territorialising music or sound and re-territorialising 'spoken ideology' or political apparatus, which can be exacerbated politically or theoretically, to take the internal discourse of Black Metal *at its word* is to insist on the *consistency* of its elements. Such a consistency is, of course, differentially and singularly articulated. One of the signs of this is the inconsistency, antagonism, and violence of the discourse between Black Metal artists; Black Metal itself is a deliberately fractured field, a field of perpetual war between different articulations of consistency. Also, the consistency between 'concrete sonic expression' and 'spoken ideology' is, no doubt, contradictory, after all what ideology is not? But what is in question is how this consistency is produced, stabilised (even if only fleetingly), and 'managed' through contradiction by Black Metal artists.

I select one singular articulation of Black Metal's political aesthetic from within this antagonistic field: the work of what we might call, in terms that would not doubt horrify him, an 'organic intellectual' of Black Metal: Sale Famine of the French Black Metal group *Peste Noire*.[1] This choice is dictated by the fact that Famine refuses any notion of the contingency of the link

---

[1] It should be noted that a Gramscian politics of hegemony has been invoked by the far right, in particular in France by Alain de Benoist, ideologue of the 'new right'. His culturalist racism and anti-Americanism bear many similarities to the views of Sale Famine, however Famine's elitism and anti-popular stance incarnate a peculiarly constrained vision of hegemony – one occult and elitist.

between Black Metal and the extreme right, instead insisting on the *necessity* of such a link. He resolutely refuses and refutes the option that would attempt to split off Black Metal as an aesthetic from the politics of the extreme right. For Famine Black Metal is, *in essence*, of the extreme right:

> To my mind, without being necessarily N[ational] S[ocialist], real Black Metal is always extreme right-wing music – be it from Asia or Latin America as extreme-right politics are not the appanage of the white race – and it is always Satanic. (Famine, *Zero Tolerance*)

In Famine's culturalist racism Black Metal is the reflection or expression of a national or territorial essence, a buried or obliterated 'essence' that must be recovered or re-articulated. At the same time this essence is always articulated with a Satanic theo-politics that blackens and corrodes what obscures this essence.

In a recent interview Famine was probed further on this statement, with the interviewer raising the case of a possible 'left-leaning' Black Metal band such as *Wolves in the Throne Room*. Famine was unequivocal in his re-iteration:

> Now, I have never heard of WOLVES IN THE THRONE ROOM, but if they praise cultural blending, common ownership and equality of all human beings, then no, they have absolutely no right to play Black Metal. They just have the right to make me laugh. (Famine, Travis interview)

Wolves in Throne Room offer what has been called a 'deep eco-metal' (Davis), and articulate a pagan and ecological world-view which is not without its own political equivocations. In fact, Famine picks up this point by noting to the interviewer that 'Ecologism was born in an extreme right-wing context ... as part of the völkish concept (the inseparable unity between folk and land, a land which should be protected as much as revered)' and, more controversially, that 'it is only later on that left-wing groups unjustly monopolized ecologistic positions' (Famine, Travis interview).

Of more importance is the marker that Famine lays down to distinguish the true aesthetico-political programme of Black Metal from any imitation: what has to be rejected is any kind of abstract levelling that would suppose constitutive equality, which threatens to implode a neo-Nietzschean politics of hierarchy and rank (we only have to recall Nietzsche's constant diatribes against the 'reactive' and levelling tendencies of democracy, Christianity, anarchism, and socialism, as forms of 'herd' or 'slave' morality). A 'left-wing Black Metal' is, for Famine, a contradiction in terms. What we have is the spectacle of a war *on* abstraction carried out by means of *further abstractions*: the abstraction of Satanism and national or territorial essence opposed to the abstractions of liberal democracy.

To dispel any potential misunderstanding Famine's negatives are my positives and, of course, from his position that automatically eliminates anything I could have to say about Black Metal. The claimed coherence of this programme dispenses with any necessity for further commentary, theoretical or otherwise, and, of course, could never be grasped from the position of the 'left-wing intellectual' – the usual abominated category of meta-abstraction. Therefore this is an immanent critique of Famine's positions through his own statements and a consideration of *Peste Noire*'s aesthetic practice. It turns on his articulation of the *integration* of the aesthetic and political to create an extreme right-wing position. Contrary to the usual sloppy correlation of aesthetic radicalism with left political radicalism, a correlation constantly belied by the history of modernism (T. S. Eliot's Maurrasian-Royalist Anglicanism, Wyndham Lewis's complex quasi-fascist anti-humanism, Ernst Jünger's national-bolshevism, Francis Stuart's nihilist ethics of abjection through collaboration), Black Metal, at least as articulated by Famine, is an aesthetic-political right-wing radicalism.

Chthonic and Telluric

What is the reason for Famine's claim of an essential articulation between Black Metal and the politics of the extreme right? It is because Black Metal articulates itself on the earth, on the chthonian and telluric, to establish its aesthetic identity:

> Black Metal is the musical memory of our bloodthirsty ancestors of blood, it is the marriage of Tradition, of old racial patrimony with fanaticism, with the rage and the

rashness of a youth now lost. It is a CHTONIAN religion: a cult of the EARTH and a return to it, therefore a nationalism; a cult of what is BELOW the earth: Hell – the adjective "chthonian" applies to the Infernal gods as well. Black Metal is a fundamentalism, a music with integrity (from Latin *integer*, complete) which helps me to remain complete in a dying world, amidst a people in decay, unworthy of its blood. It is the apology of the dark European past. It is a psychosis which helps us to flee a reality we cannot tolerate anymore. (Famine, *Zero Tolerance*)

Therefore, an authentic, real, or true Black Metal, can only, for Famine, be a Black Metal that is essentially territorial, selective, and hierarchical about the privileging of a singular and integral territory. It comes from that territory, however, occulted, and, at the same time, (re-)constructs it. The implication is that Black Metal can never exist in the abstract but only as a particular national, regional, ethnic, or racial, form. This is a politics and aesthetic of the One that only ever appears in the form of the constitutively antagonistic Two.

The result is a peculiar, to say the least, form of nationalism, although one not quite so strange when one notes the occult strains running through Nazism, fascism, and extreme right cultures:

> I am a nationalist, not a socialist . . . My two nations are: France d'Oïl and Hell. Black Metal is a double nationalism, temporal and spiritual, horizontal and vertical. 1° TEMPORAL as it is always the heritage of a BLOOD and of a material EARTH it has to worship. 2° SPIRITUAL (vertical) in that it is metaphorically a nationalism from Hell and from Darkness, an ethical and aesthetic allegiance to the Kingdom Of Evil. Of course I share (I say "I" because it is not necessarily the case for the other members) some principles of National-socialism but I reject some too. (Famine, *Zero Tolerance*)

To paraphrase Famine's axes, Black Metal articulates together a horizontal axis of history, that establishes a synedechocal continuity from the obscured European past that can be recovered only in its dispersed traces, and a vertical spatial grounding, an inverse spiritual hierarchy in neo-Platonic style, in which the 'ladder' of Being descends into the earth in terms of its participation in degrees of darkness.

This territorial politics plays an explicitly shaping role in terms of the aesthetics of Black Metal. No matter how ungrounded or abyssal this territory may appear, being 'below the earth', it underpins the essential resistance against any deterritorialising and / or democratising 'abstraction'. The very contradictions of *Peste Noire*'s aesthetic, its own fractured and strange parataxis of cultural elements, are related precisely to this spatio-temporal territorialisation:

> As far as the traditional/non-traditional contrast is concerned, I would say Beauty, Grandeur, Nobleness emanate when PN evoke the European PAST (which explains that melancholy, which is nostalgia) with a Black Metal in accordance with our forefathers's tradition (BURZUM, MÜTIILATION, VLAD TEPES). Hatred, terror, DISORDER, madness break out when we conjure up the CURRENT democratic world. Naturally that disorder is expressed in forms which are less conventional. (Famine, *Zero Tolerance*)

The irony is that the aesthetic elements of Black Metal most likely to appeal to the left, or left-leaning, cultural critic – its use of 'forms which are less conventional', its evocation of terror or madness – are simply contingent elements that result from the mimetic parsing of the fallen world of modernity which Famine despises.

Evan Calder Williams notes that Peste Noire's album *Ballade cuntre lo anemi francor* (2009) plays between the 'impossible return' to a lost past and 'the bare noise and pulse of a modern world' ('Misanthropy'). This is often played out in the contrast between an 'angelic' female vocal, and the 'demonic' Gollum-like rasping and wheezing of Famine or, in the track 'La Mesniee Mordrissoire', between Famine's voice and the harmonious martial male voice. At the level of the lyrics and the music it comes in the deliberate provocation of corrupting traditional military and royalist songs with singing the praises of Satan and the recognisable, although inimitable, elements of Black Metal. The brief (1.29) track 'Concerto pour Cloportes', for example, would not, out of context, necessarily be recognisable as 'Black Metal': introduced with the sound of rewinding tape, its hiss-laden piano track is overlayed with a female 'aaahh' that is distorted into screeching, and ends with a mock Satanic laughter. The album has several of these 'inserts', like the wistful Church-organ style track 'Vespre', coupled to extended tracks like 'Rance Black Metal de France' – with *Peste Noire*'s usual soaring guitar work, Famine's rasping vocal, and even birdsong (perhaps an unconscious snub to *Wolves in the Throne Room?*).

This aesthetic is articulated in the form of a radical splitting. It is an album of deliberate contradiction and aesthetic tension, so 'Black Metal' we could say that, as Famine intimates, he no longer has to conform to Black Metal.[2] But does this splitting allow us to divide One into Two? Can we recuperate the staging of the 'bare noise and pulse of the modern world' as the nihilist critique of what Badiou calls 'capitalo-parliamentarianism' without the embarrassing archaic fascist

---

[2] Famine states that the next *Peste Noire* album will be 'pure reggae' (Travis Interview), inhabiting his usual mode of deliberate provocation, but also implying his own ability to define a true Black Metal, in quasi-Duchampian mode, as whatever he nominates.

nostalgia? For *Peste Noire* and Sale Famine we cannot split this splitting: the antagonistic One of Black Metal is composed through the permanent clash between the 'angelic' or 'virile' elements of the lost / impossible past and the 'noise' that is representative of a fallen modern world – this quasi-'dialectical' tension cannot be divided again. Famine's 'boyscout Satanism' (Travis interview) – Sieg Hell instead of Sieg Heil, and Nietzschean übermensch sodomy – is predicated on the retention of an aesthetic and political 'fractured unity'.

Cultural Partisan

To specify more closely this imbrication of politics and aesthetics I want to detour through Carl Schmitt's work *Theory of the Partisan* (1963). Schmitt is attempting to articulate the disturbance caused by the figure of the partisan in the usual state-logic of warfare, in which the partisan creates an indistinction between the conventional combatant and civilian. In Schmitt's analysis the 'good' partisan is the one that retains their telluric character: 'He defends a piece of land with which he has an autochthonous relation.' (*Partisan* 92) For this reason the partisan, although disturbing to the usual order of the 'friend-enemy' distinction by which Schmitt defines the space of the political, remains within it by having a 'real enemy' – one territorially defined. The 'bad' partisan, which Schmitt unsurprisingly identifies with communist militancy, has no telluric grounding and instead generalises their struggle to create an 'absolute enemy'. In this case 'the partisan also became absolute and a bearer of an absolute enmity.' (*Partisan* 93)

The political stakes of the partisan turn on the question of figuration and abstraction. Schmitt has to integrate the reality of the partisan within his conception of politics and war, as dictated by the necessity of the distinction between the friend and the enemy, by policing the status of the partisan as still, in however an attenuated a fashion, linked to the earth (hence resistant to abstraction). The partisan must form the figure of the (potential) enemy. In contrast the communist partisan, linked only to the internationalised militancy of the Party, threatens to undo this grounding by embracing equalitarian abstraction and so is radically de-figured and dispersed. The horror of this absolute abstraction is correlated to perpetual war and absolute violence.

Of course it might be thought to unduly flatter Famine to regard *Peste Noire* as a 'partisan group', although it seems to be congruent with their own self-image. In the context of *Ballade Cuntre lo Anemi Francor* we witness the aesthetic and political construction of the figure of the 'enemy'. Schmitt, in Nietzschean fashion, regards the figure of the enemy as the shape or configuration of our own question: 'The enemy is who defines me. That means *in concreto*: only my brother can challenge me and only my brother can be my enemy.' (*Partisan*

85 n89) In Schmitt the figure of the enemy also has a pacifying function: the construction politics around the friend-enemy distinction is to define ourselves and also to regard our enemy as an enemy, rather than as someone to be exterminated. If the partisan threatens to unbind this function, their telluric and political grounding in a defensive national struggle is the means Schmitt uses to retain the partisan within the *nomos* of the earth.

In the case of Famine and *Peste Noire* we could argue that their own telluric identification with a defensive national cultural struggle performs a similar function. The vituperative construction of the figure of the plural 'enemies' of France gives a figural coherence to their cultural struggle. They try to remain partisans in the positive sense Schmitt gives this function, and so 'remain true to the earth'. This project is, however, in tension with the fragmentation and dispersion the plural indicates. Here the disturbance lies on the side of what is being struggled against – the capitalist effects and forces of real abstraction, which are also missing from Schmitt's account of the partisan. These uprooting and emptying dynamics of disembedding and deterritorialisation are, precisely, the effect of social relations and resist localisation in particular figural enemies. The threat is not here an abstract politics of equality, although, almost quaintly, Famine still seems to regard this as on the table. Instead, it is the abstractive politics of equality of 'one market under God', to use Thomas Frank's felicitous phrase, that unbinds the consistency of the figure of the 'enemy'.

The result is that we can interpret this singular instance of the politics of Black Metal as an instance of *resistance*, but of a particular type. Famine/*Peste Noire* try to inhabit, metaphorically, the position of Schmitt's telluric partisan to give form and figure to their enemies. The escape of their 'enemies', due to the de-figuring effects of capital, constantly evacuates this project of content. This draining makes it possible to locate this aesthetic politics within a category of postmodern parody or blank irony – hence not to be taken seriously. Famine himself endorses this by his reference to the album as work of 'boyscout Satanism' and indicates the necessity of mockery and humour to the project: '*Ballade* ... is a very joyous, colourful and carnival like album.' (Travis interview) The error here is to assume the correlation of the politics of the extreme right with a po-faced seriousness, ignoring the fact that, as Famine insists, such a political aesthetic can easily embrace the carnivalesque.

It is not that there are no effects of irony, parody, or humour at work, and not that they are merely side effects of a ludicrous anachronistic meta-fascism. Instead they are deliberate, but also necessary, because of the effects of the 'resistance' to the cultural framing of capitalist real abstraction – to put it most economically, the effect of the value-form of the commodity, which is radically indifferent to content. In the face of this fundamental indifference it comes as no surprise that that *this* enemy (capitalism) cannot give us self-definition, and the figural struggle to embody such an enemy by Famine / *Peste Noire* is endless and endlessly failing. The humour, which is largely sardonic, falls exactly on the realism of the futility of this struggle, which does not prevent or disable this cultural 'resistance' but is its very motor. I would also add that there is real anguish here, whatever the parodic desires of Famine, or the parodic effects of the socio-economic forms of the law of value. His is a political / cultural desperation, although one that certainly, and necessarily, takes malignant telluric forms.

Sharpening the Contradictions

For Famine and his articulation of Black Metal One necessarily divides into Two – this politics of the One cannot simply claim or recover the One as given, but only ever articulate such a 'One' in the form of the necessarily antagonistic Two. Replying to my reading of the politics of Black Metal Evan Calder Williams focuses on this point. Refining his earlier model he insists that there can be no separation of 'the musical wheat from the crypto-fascist chaff', but instead that we must recognise that Black Metal operates through a constitutive impurity ('headless'). Black Metal is a *Kampfplatz*, a fissured site of 'constant return to buried antagonisms', that tries to produce the clearing away of a final war of Armageddon but which can only constantly re-iterate an 'impure apocalypse' ('headless'). The antagonism of the 'divided One' is posed against any possible return to, or retroactive recomposition of, the One as such. In the manner of the sorcerer's apprentice Black Metal unleashes forces it cannot control and which return to destroy itself in an acephalic auto-consumption.

Certainly Black Metal is 'composed of antinomies' ('headless'), and bears witness to a hatred of the present. The critical question remains whether this results in self-destruction, or whether these antinomies can be stabilised within an aestheticised politics? Contra Williams, it may not simply be that 'Black Metal is the failure of dialectical reason, and for that reason, it is a razor sharp capture of the stuck-record world it rejects.' ('headless') Obviously it is not trying to articulate 'reason' – the dominant tone of Black Metal is deliberate 'irrationalism' – but a certain coherence remains in this 'stalled dialetic', which is formed in the necessary *linkage* and 'balancing' of the antinomies. Certainly the 'pure' negativity of Black Metal does refuse the usual forms of dialectical 'synthesis', or retroaction. It refuses any model of historical advance, even one, as in Marx, that proceeds by the bad side. Obsessed with history as site of war it conducts what Marx calls, in a different context, a 'world-historical necromancy' (147). But this dialectic of resurrection and recovery operates in the form of re-iterated antagonism as division or splitting of abstraction that dreams of a 'concrete' moment it can never recover.

Despite the refusal of the naïve model of the dialectic as thesis-antithesis-synthesis, Black Metal still operates with the clashing elements it deploys to produce its own virtual 'negation of the negation' as affirmation. The permanence of conflict attests to the ever-receding utopian hope of the abolishing of the present, whilst also preserving a consistent and stabilised enmity to that present that gives the supplement of identity and integration – the affirmation of Black Metal as the centre of the whirlwind. The virtuality of this integration lies in its deferral, but remains as a virtual 'vanishing point', a hermeneutic horizon, that refuses self-dissemination. On its own criteria should Black Metal triumph as the recovery of a true aesthetic-politics of the 'impossible past' it would then disappear – we can imagine *Ballade Cuntre lo Anemi Francor* re-recorded or edited so it is without the elements of the 'fallen world'. The fact that this does not and cannot occur is what *maintains* Black Metal as an abstract aestheticisation of politics in the service of a dialectic that can only produce further 'concrete abstractions'.

The second critical point made by Williams is that the 'negative dialectics' of Black Metal contains the pluralised trace of a utopian articulation of the dream of collective militancy. In a similar fashion to Fredric Jameson's noting that fascism and Nazism still hold the utopian trace of the dream of community, obviously in the completely degraded form of a national-racial 'organicism', Williams suggests that Black Metal holds the utopian trace of a negativity of group militancy. Again the antagonistic Two ruptures the One: not a *wolf* in the throne room, but *wolves* (a Deleuzo-Guattarian pack, persumably, rather than the Oedipalised family of wolves) ('headless'). Certainly, as Williams does, we can stress that Black Metal deploys a 'corrosive negativity which takes as its first target the very individualism black metal reifies' ('headless'), but we could also argue that this Stirnerite dismantling of the ego can easily be re-territorialised. A politicised dissolution of the ego can serve to recompose a reified and purified abstraction of the elite group or community (as implied by Stirner's 'union of egoists'). We could recall Freud's haute-liberal hostility to just such dissolutions of the ego in the crowd precisely because such dissolutions depend on the figure of the leader or the One. This is exactly the point made by Famine: 'Through P[este] N[oire] I created an IDEAL and LESS FRAGILE ego' (*Zero Tolerance* interview). This ego is 'Ideal' because aestheticised, an auto-constitution of the new self, and 'less fragile', 'because thanks to PN I break free from my little and ephemeral body to become incarnate somewhere else'

(*Zero Tolerance* interview). It is through art that Famine claims to achieve 'a noble existence' (*Zero Tolerance* interview), in conformity to Nietzsche's model of the ego as a 'work of art', and the auto-constitution of the self as One through fragmentation and dissolution – 'which helps me to remain complete in a dying world' (Famine, *Zero Tolerance*).

In question here is the particular form of group militancy Black Metal articulates, which may be plural but is organised around integrity, however delayed and deferred – in fact an integrity constituted *through* dissolution. Again, rather than taking unbinding as a given, or the true dynamic of Black Metal, I would suggest, in line with its own discourse, that we take seriously that this unbinding serves another binding. The resistance to abstraction takes the form of a figural abstraction of the concrete 'ego' – exalted as the 'Unique One'. Plurality takes place through and with the 'group' as pack, but re-singularised by the 'integrity' of the group. Black Metal is by no means alone in such methods of policing the group or community and, of course, virtually all subcultures, for reasons of group integrity, delineate 'true' members from 'false': the 'hardcore' from mere 'weekenders', 'thugs for life' from mere fake gangsters, 'true school' from wannabes, and so on. Often, but of course not always, this particular policing function is overlaid or overdetermined in Black Metal by a politico-aesthetic coding from the extreme right. This is the dialectic of Stirner and Nietzsche – the elective and hierarchised 'union of egoists' that subtract themselves from what they regard as the false abstractions of 'mere humanity' or 'democratic subjectivity' to deliver themselves to the separated and hierarchical 'concrete community'.

The acepahlic nature of Black Metal, or its acephalic tendency that Williams' notes, does not solve the political and aesthetic problem. Of course the implicit reference here is to Bataille, and notably his constant struggle to articulate a chthonic politics that could seize such energies from fascism without recomposing a singular sovereign heterogeneity. The difficulty, which Bataille well recognised, and which aroused Walter Benjamin's suspicions, is the ability to definitively split such a politics from fascist or Nazi articulations of sovereign heterogeneity. The invocation of 'the sheer nihilistic impurity of the din, crushing the possibility of any individual sustaining itself as a discrete positivity' ('headless') underestimates this difficulty, and reinstates a saving split of the 'good' in Black Metal from the 'bad'. Instead, not simply to condemn Black Metal but rather to simply recognise its political stakes, this articulation is closer and more essential than the indication of contradiction can handle. What Williams calls a 'tainted proximity' ('headless') is exactly the form and consistency that I have endeavoured to reconstruct, as the necessary measure of the actual and potential politics of Black Metal.

'Habitués of the chthonic forces of terror'

It should be evident that, as Walter Benjamin long ago pointed out, the division of aesthetics and politics cannot grasp the articulations of an aestheticisation of politics. The specificity of Benjamin's identification of fascism with such an aestheticisation, and his opposition to that of a communist politicisation of aesthetics, is rendered both problematic and general by the aestheticisation of social existence by post-war capitalism. In fact, we could argue that this is why Famine and *Peste Noire*'s aestheticisation of politics figures itself as a kind of ironic meta-fascism – precisely because the grounding gesture of its own collapsing together of the aesthetic and the political is no longer, if it ever was, the singular purview of fascism and Nazism. It is here that its 'integrity' fails.

And yet Benjamin's initial diagnosis still has resonances for the analysis of the politics of Black Metal. In his article 'Theories of German Fascism', prior to the formulations in 'The Work of Art' essay, Benjamin analysed the vitalist-nationalist mysticism of Ernst Jünger and his circle. His characterisation of these 'habitués of the chthonic forces of terror' who peddle 'sinister runic humbug' ('Theories' 128), correlates with Black Metal's similar fetishisation of war, radicalised nihilism, and an extreme right-wing politics that articulates itself in modes similar to that of the extreme left (pace Jünger's 'national Bolshevism'). Benjamin's point, relevant to Black Metal, is that it is perfectly possible to have a consistent politics, in this case fascist, articulated through a radicalised modernist aesthetic; more precisely that fascist politics *is* aesthetic. This articulation turns on the vaolrisation of 'form-giving power', derived from Spengler and Nietzsche, that aestheticises politics – with political subsumed within the *gesamtkunstwerk*.

Benjamin acidly argued that the fetishisation of technology and war 'as an incisive magical turning point' ignores the fact it was an 'everyday actuality' ('Theories' 128). Much the same rejoinder could be made to Black Metal, especially in the actual context of neo-colonial war as 'everyday actuality' in Iraq and Afghanistan. At the same time, however, we must also recognise the different conditions of this articulation. The aestheticisation and abstraction of social existence by capitalism in the time of real subsumption is what gives the aesthetic politics of Black Metal its mixture of pathos and bathos. The struggle to pose 'form-giving power' against the power of real abstractions creates particular forms of aesthetic politics that cannot simply be identified with 'classical' fascism and Nazism, although, as I have noted, they have new malignant resonances in our global political and economic space that still falls back onto tellurian and nativist re-territorialisations. My point is not a falsely inflationary one, with Black Metal as the viral carrier of a 'new Fascism', but neither is it one that stresses dismissive complacency or the ease of extracting from Black Metal a new 'purified' and acceptable aesthetic radicalism. Instead, it is to stress the functional coherent incoherence of Black Metal, its constitutive impurity, as its mechanism.

Certainly I have only focused on one singular instance of the politics of Black Metal and I am not taking this instance as strictly metonymic of all Black Metal positions and politics. It is, however, symptomatic and revealing because of its explicit form and ambition, as well as, why not?, its aesthetic success. This is a politics which conforms to Badiou's analysis of the 'passion for the real' and the twentieth century as the century of war and scission – a stalled dialectic of the division of the One into an antagonistic Two that can never stabilise. The aesthetic of *Peste Noire* cannot be separated from this antagonism, but inhabits it as the effect of fusion of the aesthetic and the political to give figuration to an always elusive 'enemy'. Of course, contra

Famine's desire, the abstractive figural desire of his work makes it available to those non-telluric and non-chthonic enemies he professes to hate – he would, of course, despise this analysis. This is not to take the easy path of postmodern 'everyone reads in their own way', or limitless politics of re-inscription that would license a reading 'for socialism'. Instead, I have tried to take seriously a depth of commitment, which I unequivocally reject politically, in the cultural articulation of the political and aesthetic. I remain, however, one of the enemies of France.

References

Badiou, Alain, *The Century* [2005], trans., with commentary and notes, Alberto Toscano (Cambridge, UK, and Malden, MA: Polity, 2007).

Benjamin, Walter, 'Theories of German Fascism', trans. Jerolf Wikoff, *New German Critique* 17 (Spring 1979): 120-128.

Birk, Nathan T., "Interview with La Sale Famine of Peste Noire", *Zero Tolerance*, <http://www.gutsofdarkness.com/_files/pdf/2007_02_fevrier.pdf> [accessed 24 August 2009].

Davis, Erik, 'Deep Eco-Metal', *Slate*, November 13 2007, <http://www.slate.com/id/2177883/> [accessed 8 January 2009].

Marx, Karl, 'The Eighteenth Brumaire of Louis Bonaparte', in *Surveys from Exile*, ed. and trans. David Fernbach (Harmondsworth: Penguin, 1973), pp.143-249.

Nietzsche, Friedrich, *The Will to Power*, trans. W. Kaufmann and R. J. Hollingdale, ed. W. Kaufmann (New York: Vintage, 1968).

Schmitt, Carl, *Theory of the Partisan*, trans. G. L. Ulmen (New York: Telos Publishing, 2007).

Stirner, Max, *The Ego and His Own*, trans. Steven T. Byington (New York: Ben R. Tucker Publisher, 1907). Available from The Egoist Archive:
<http://www.nonserviam.com/egoistarchive/stirner/TheEgo.pdf> [accessed 24 August 2009].

Travis (Diabolical Conquest), 'Interview with Famine of the French Black Metal band Peste Noire', *Diabolical Conquest: Underground Extreme Metal Webzine*, August 12 2009,
<http://www.diabolicalconquest.com/interviews/peste_noire_english.htm> [accessed 18 August 2009].

Williams, Evan Calder, 'Three hours (misanthropy)', *Socialism and/or barbarism* blog, 9 June 2009,
<http://socialismandorbarbarism.blogspot.com/2009/06/three-hours-misanthropy.html> [accessed 17 August 2009].

___, 'The headless horseman of the apocalypse', *Socialism and/or barbarism* blog, 14 December 2009,
<http://socialismorbarbarism.blogspot.com/2009/12/headless-horsemen-of-apocalypse.html> [accessed 22 December 2009].

Discography

Peste Noire, *Ballade Cuntre lo Anemi Francor*, De Profundis, France, 2009.

THE HEADLESS HORSEMEN OF THE APOCALYPSE
Evan Calder Williams

At its raspy start, black metal begins with the obscene purity of the end: with *Pure Fucking Armageddon*, the title of Mayhem's first demo from 1986. Of course, black metal never really begins. It's always been out of time, eternally out of joint with a world it hates, even as it cannot leave that world behind. But if we take one among many points of departure, it may as well be this one, from the good old dark days, a declaration of where to go from there. The name itself is a founding gesture, and we take it as such, as a formal template and an injunction to be fulfilled: black metal will be *pure fucking Armageddon*. Or, to specify, it will operate beneath that constitutive fantasy, and it will be constituted by how it keeps reproducing its distance from such a fantasy. That is, it promises itself as *pure* and as *Armageddon*, even as it dismantles any possibility of ever being either. Rather, it is *impure fucking apocalypse*. (As for the *fucking* issue, that remains spot-on and relatively uncomplicated. To follow Sargeist, it's the difference between "black murder" and "Black Fucking Murder." It is one of BM's great modifiers, endlessly recombined to specify the blackness and metalness of things, ranking up there with *necro, grim, dark, cold, Northern, pestilent, Satanic,* and in certain periods, *Carpathian* and *Transylvanian*.)

Above all, black metal is war. It is fought under the banner of a desired final war to come: the striving march from *impure apocalypse of the present* to the *pure Armageddon of the end*. To leave behind the messiness and imprecision of the Now, not by dreaming about the future but through a constant return to buried antagonisms (i.e. Satan's alternate history of the world, flammable churches, pagan knowledge, ancestral legacies). To become a fierce and directed manifestation of shared hatred toward the assumed positivity of what the order of the day is (i.e. Christianity, liberal democracy, multi-nationalism, warm weather, false metal). And above all, to know finally, once and for all, what the hell to do with that hellish hatred of the present.

What is the difference between *apocalypse* and *Armageddon*? Apocalypse is a mode of vision, a process, a revelation of what is hidden, of the unclear, of the undifferentiated. To be properly black metal about it all, if the veil is lifted, the revelation is of the cursed impure that could not be grasped in this rational order. A black sun casts different light, and the growing shadows reveal only what has been hidden in plain sight all along. Consequently, apocalypse is not the end but the beginning of the end. In revealing the hidden, it starts the process of resorting, reorienting, struggling through the mess of what has been shown and now won't go away. The apocalypse leads to the post-apocalypse. Contrary to this, Armageddon is the *site of the terminal end*. It is not the end itself (not the eschaton), but the battlefield on which the final confrontation will be fought between the differentiated enemies, now clear and "pure" in their opposition.

What does this have to do with black metal, or with Mayhem's demo title as a founding gesture? It is to think of black metal as a battlefield from the start, as a phenomenal working through of that imagined site, that promised zone of contestation where the contemporary world is swept away to confront the old antagonisms. But against its endless stated reiterations, the battlefield – and the war itself – is not purified location of Armageddon. It is rather the total messiness of the impure apocalypse and the strewn landscape. A total, unceasing war not between enemies grouped on opposite sides of the final Two, but a war to try and draw forth a Two, to rediscover the possibility of antagonism and movement in the permanent fog and jumble of the present.

So stands black metal, pulled in two again and again, without enlightenment or escape. Composed of antinomies that do not, against all odds, cancel each other out, supersede through redouble negation, or advance through combination. Hence the absence of the usual dialectical suspects: not void, not synthesis, not the *not-not* of the negation of the negation. It is a blurring, buzzing, necessarily late 20th century electric mess (the howling sound of global infrastructure and transmission), but it can only think itself as the cruel and nostalgic articulation of a local heritage of ancient earth and cold blood. And it is the strident forging of the horde's shared total enmity, yet which can only make itself appear as the individualistic work of loner devotees of Satan with too many crossbows and a love of strolling in the woods. In other words, pulled somewhere between a willingness to be unapologetic enemies of what the world has become, a deep and arcane goofiness riddled with stone-faced mediocre nationalism, a sonic blast, and a melancholia of the unwanted, black metal takes formless shape. Bellicosity and dysphoria, raging mess and lost purity.

The point of this investigation isn't to redeem this or iron out its contradictions. It certainly isn't to separate the musical wheat from the crypto-Fascist chaff. Rather, it's to dwell in the utter overdetermination and to start to grasp, as black metal itself does raggedly, what can never be separated or cleared away. Black metal is the failure of dialectical reason. And for that reason, it is a razor sharp capture of the stuck-record world it rejects, even as it cannot think beyond it. All that cohabits impossibly cannot be separated, and it therefore must be a site of war, a contested site of destruction without clean-up or resolution. That which is negated sticks around in its own negation, and it starts to reek. Restless decay that does not fade away, but only gets louder. Nihil unbound and bound to fail.

What, then, is black metal if not a minor totality itself: overdetermination that does not cancel out, the impossible whole that lumbers on? Following Benjamin Noys's application of the Schmittian logic of the partisan (according to which the "bad partisan" produces the end of discernible enemies by making enmity absolute and universal), this *bellum omnium contra omnes* is not a war between discrete individuals all against all.[1] It is the war fought between two totalities, between black metal's endless antagonism and liberal capitalism's eternal present.

The specific condition on which black metal is staked is indeed that of the *militant anti-contemporary partisan*, of how to transition from

---

[1] This essay should be read alongside – and against – Noys's essay in this volume that incorporates a response to the version of my essay given at the symposium. Our thinking has developed in tandem, via a shared concern with the political consequences of black metal and a fundamental disagreement about what can come out of its deadlock of stuck negation. His piece raises a number of considerable objections to my work, too many to address here. My next work of black metal theory, which further develops the move from acephale to cephalophore, will continue this debate, to ask more particularly: *can negation and enmity be blurred? Must all principles of integral collectivity be taken as fascist?*

melancholic dejection of the Now to furious rejection in the name of Then (as interstitial moment of lost pagan battle or future Ragnarök). The lyrics of Vordr's "From Ruins to Victorious Triumph," screeched over its D-beat stomp and churning fuzz, precisely map this envisioned arc. From "*I do not care / For the earthly pleasures / Of humanity / I couldn't care less / I couldn't care less*" to "*Along with the unseen / I shall rise / From ruins to victorious triumph / My time is yet to come.*" This may start with the frosty and properly misanthropic turn away from the accepted sphere of the human, yet it still remains trapped in the potential realm of the petulant bedroom shut-in, the dysphoric who dwells in the petty pleasures of feigning disinterest in the earthly sphere. That is, who prefers to stay home and out of the fray. But the point of transition is truly apocalyptic: to rise with the "unseen", the impure, the undifferentiated. It begins in the ruins, not in the lyrical twilight solitude of the allegorical death's head but from the ruined ground, if not from farther below, and the accumulated broken weight of past struggle and constant failure.

From this sense of the *where*, we should venture three further questions about this war of fractured and antinomian totality. When does it take place? Who is fighting and leading the battle? What kind of war is it?

To start with the temporal dimension, the *when* of the war: *black metal is the restaging of a past war that was to have happened yet which missed its chance.* (The beginning of the end that didn't take, the failed start.) If, returning to that Vordr line, "my time is yet to come," black metal hinges on the incapacity – and fury at that incapacity – of that time ever coming to be. Apocalyptically, it is caught between imminent and immanent eschaton: it predicts and describes a final battle, yet it grasps that final battle as one which has been there all along. Out of this noisy deadlock, it reaches in one of two directions. Either it hails toward a past that wasn't there (the time of lost telluric tradition, to be approached gnostically or through embedded folk traditions), or it approaches a stance outside of human time (the sublime of Nature, the atemporal adversity of Satan, the anti-thought of nothing itself). Either the nostalgia of degraded purity, or the purity of the concept of the inhuman itself. What binds the two together, even as it remains beyond the explicit purview of black metal thought, is an underground awareness that the banality and brutality of the contemporary world is both intolerable and inescapable. And furthermore, that it is far worse than any necrotic pestilential midnight hell swarm ever conjured by Norwegians. Therein the desperation of black metal vocals: it's just the howl of the thought that this is at once the worst of all possible worlds and the only possible world. The point, then, is to find a mode of virulent resistance and acid bath negativity, and it can only ever come from afar. Not from the immanent same of the present, not from the imminent difference of the future, but from an absent past.

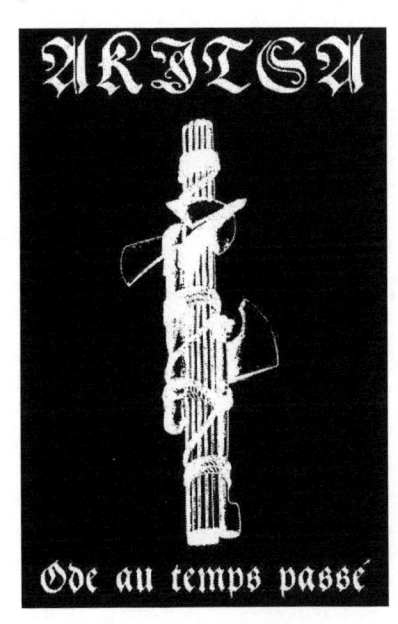

Who fights this war, and who leads them? Despite the constant lip service to the affective portrait of the loner individual, we should venture the contrary: *black metal has no individuals, and it has no leaders.* At times, it has nations, folklores, heritages, and kingdoms. It has pasts. But above all, it has that corrosive negativity which takes as its first target the very individualism black metal reifies. This is no ideological swindle or disavowal. It is there in relentless repetition of the imagery (hordes, legions, swarms, wolves, barbarians, armies of the night, cults, fasces), and it is there in the music, in the sheer nihilistic impurity of the din, crushing the possibility of any individual sustaining itself as a discrete positivity. The war by the human in the name of the inhuman devours the former. And no *one* can lead, no one deserves such a reward of being worth a damn in the face of it all. Instead, it is the sovereignty of the partisan group, the collected enemies of the world, however regionally bound they may be. In this way, despite its moronic and frequent attempts to be Fascist and despite the fact that we should wage total war against all such attempts, it never can be. It is perhaps always marked by its tainted proximity and distance from it, the negative term persisting even in absence: all non-Nazi black metal is still NSNSBM (not so National Socialist black metal). But its contested and scarred ground remains the battlefield of the impure and the undifferentiated. *It can never leave this, and it doesn't want to.* If we do talk about blood and land, it can only be a feeling of blood, a cold comportment against the warm torpor of the capitalist present, not a genetic coldness shared by the northern tribes. And it can only be a land to be taken en masse, not to be rescued from a unstained past. Black metal dreams a sovereign, and, in the next breath, severs his head to spatter the blood across all. What remains are the headless horsemen of the apocalypse, the acephalic leaders of a chiefless crowd marching off to permanent war.

But to speak of beheading, one must ask: what happens to the head? And whose was it to start? For the acephale (the headless) is the ground of black metal, its fundamental and unstable condition, but also what dooms it to both its fascism-in-spite-of-itself and to the lingering sense of the bad faith to not follow through on its convictions. The acephale needs to be taken as a first gesture, not as a permanent condition. Not in order to recuperate or excuse, neither to denigrate nor to valorize, but to see that the act of becoming headless opens the way for the second gesture, that of the cephalophore, the head-bearer, the one defined not by the condition of being without head but by the *act* of picking the head back up.[2] "Head" here should be taken in its full range, for the acephalic is a fantasy both of the leaderless (the "body" of the people rules alone, brought about by that revolutionary act of beheading the sovereign, materially or in principle) and of the irrational (headless, the body rules in its

---

[2] The notion of the cephalophore came to me via Nicola Masciandaro, who has considered it extensively. I raise it here briefly, holding it out more as a gesture for the next essay to come, which will take up from here. If this essay is on the acephalic condition of black metal, part two will be on the cephalophoric horizon.

singularity and decides on the basis of the affective, and phenomenal, taking on unreason as its shared principle). As such, the acephalic condition of black metal must surpass itself and extend this to a total condition. It isn't enough to remove the leader and imagine the hard collective – of cold Northern sovereigns to be – merely touched by this act of negation, for the outcome is one of three inevitabilities:

> Resubmission to the bellicose repetition of the act (which is perhaps fine with black metal, at its most raging-in-place).

A slide toward the directionless muddled chaos of a crowd of loners.

> Most disturbingly and more determinately fascist, the elevation of a new leader capable of both retroactively verifying the absent and deferred integration of the mass, as well as yoking concretely together the necessarily linked and distanced practices of politics and aesthetics.[3]

In other words, the crowd itself must not only sever all. It must also pick up the pieces after. And more than that, to realize that the destructive undercurrent of this is above all an affective stance and an aesthetic tendency. The heads are already

---

[3] I hold out, however, that we need to investigate further the consequences of such a leader being one of two options harder to fit into a cleanly Fascist sphere. Namely, Satan (who never shows up when he's supposed to) or the mass cephalophoric subject (which is the collective principle of making practicable the after-the-fact of the Ragnarök-esque event).

severed, reason cast to the ground. Black metal makes appear as decision what is in truth a general state of affairs, not just of its imagined post-apocalypse but of the systemic chaos and non-direction of the contemporary world. Hence the performative theatricality: the head already removed, the axe's swing is a magician's trick, tracing the negative space there all along between the body and the head.

For to remain in the acephalic is to rest in one of two unacceptable options, each of which can then go in one of two ways. There can be an acephalic leader, which means either heterogeneous sovereignty (the elevation of a singular, irrational, decisionist leader to prop up the whole collapsing sphere of homogeneous and ordered life) or that crowd of individuals against rational leadership only because it is the wrong kind of rational leadership (i.e. liberal, plural, "diverse" and contemporary, rather than something more metal, European, singular, and ancient). And there can be an acephalic crowd, either stuck in waiting for a properly headed leader to emerge and give direction, or caught in riotous, irrational, affective bloodbath, stumbling and flailing around, confusing an attack on totality with an attack on everything and anything within reach, wounding itself as it goes.

But despite its recurrent anti-intellectualism and penchant for uncritical reenactment of stale dark vitalist tropes, black metal is smarter than it thinks. Appropriately for its Satanic grounding, it shares much with the integral atheism of de Sade: to take on abstraction and the generic, you have to do so on its own terms. In other words, you can't afford to throw away the head. It must be picked up, made open use of. Not to resuture a lost order to the mediated despair of the present, not t0 stitch the head back on. Rather, to make its absence and dislocation visible, to make something better of the inherited atrocity. To be sure, a cephalophoric leader could be no better than the acephalic, now holding up the head as proof of martyrdom (*how I've suffered for you*), reconciliation (*I know you were mad when you cut off my head, but I forgive you and come back whole and wholly different, ready for hope and change*), or permanence (*cut my head off, it won't do any good, you're stuck with me, foolish sheep*). And so the requisite fourth here, and the possible way for black metal out of its stalemate of wishing to lose its head even while it won't let it go, is the cephalophoric group. Headless one and all, they hold heads aloft, not sure to whom each belonged in the first place. Removed, yes, but redistributed: the general intellect and spheres of abstraction are severed decisively from their "natural" connection, and then turned to other ends. Of course, black metal doesn't reach here. It remains the stumbling din, and the bad faith of a rational proclamation of irrational singularity, of the acephale who knows better. The question to be held out before us, like a disjointed head, is what can be gained and seen otherwise, the sight and praxis to be found in becoming literally wrong-headed.

Finally, what kind of war? *It is the war of totality against itself.* Always caught mid-flight, between the headless and the head-bearing, black metal is the negative insistence: no transcendence, no redemption, no revelation. Yet this negation does not hack and slash open a clear spot on Armageddon's plains. It does not allow for apocalyptic *krisis*, the clarity of separation and judgment, or for the understanding of what the battle has been about from the start, the secret history of the world made bloody well clear. Black metal is the obsessive yearning lunge toward such clarity, and it is the abortive impossibility of reaching it. What is all this desire for, and talk about, *purity* but the mislocation of real lust for *clarity*, for knowing who your enemies are? Because it knows, with imperfect gnosis, that the enemy is something immense and diffuse, and so it becomes that enemy itself, singing of the far-off End's clarity with the voice of autophagic contradiction.

And so it is sonically. It is a static war, restless and bristling, but it is also a war of static. A war both *by* and *against* static: the buzzing howl nearly drowned out in the constant growl of late capitalist totality. For despite its hailing back to the absent origin, black metal is the sound – and politics, for there is no divorcing of the two – of this infernal and eternal present turned up and back on itself. It is feedback literalized. The pickups register, amplify, and ramp up to overdriven fever pitch all the circuits of the world order, the pathways of circulation, the electrified hum of production and calculation. And above all, the inhuman voice of the once-human nearly lost in the roar.

Black metal brings out the deadlock that was there from the start, between individuation and totality, and between a principle of negativity and the inertia of the positive. If the fantasmatic condition on which black metal is staked is indeed that of *militancy*, its impossible solution is *collective militancy*: that alone can make the deadlock tremor.

To strike a totality by becoming a negative totality together, not the smooth individual rods of a fascist bundle, but a storm and swarm of the *anti*. To take on the abortive passage of the apocalyptic as mandate and injunction, not to do right, but to do wrongly to a wrong world. Never to fall into sadness or dejection at the prospect, but to rage with joy. Therein we catch the crooked grin of the misanthrope who finds his grim horde, the smile hidden behind the shared illusion of non-pleasure. And above all, to do this together. To become totally singular and negatively universal is to take on the acephalic mess that we are – by becoming cephalophoric, by not just severing but by picking up the pieces – and to undo the idiocy of any nostalgia for a purer time. Only from there do we forge Luciferian, not Satanic, collectivity: knowing very well that we can't take the throne, and doing it all the same. Such is the decisive, intervening core of black metal refusal, for better or for worse. There's a reason that it isn't *Wolf in the Throne Room*. It's *Wolves*, that strident, impure, unwanted pack of inhuman negativity, the absent crown shattered into knives for and against all.

MEANINGFUL LEANING MESS
Brandon Stosuy

The following's a brief excerpt from a larger work in progress, a still-untitled oral history of American black metal I plan to publish in book form. A different excerpt ran under the title "A Blaze In The North American Sky" in the July/August 2008 issue of *The Believer*. Matt Luem gave an oral presentation of an untitled California-themed excerpt at Joe's Pub, NYC, in August 2009. The below is a slightly expanded version of what I read at Hideous Gnosis.

///

Dagon, Inquisition: The lineage of black metal doesn't begin in one country and with one band. There is this romance that one band/one man/one nation started it all. Wrong. It was a collective campaign during the late '70s/early 80s, throughout Europe and the United States that "morphed" into what later became the Norwegian scene and gave us what we know as today's Black metal

Andee, Aquarius Records/tUMULt: If you asked most black metal musicians from the U.S. I'm pretty sure most of them would cite the Scandinavian bands as the true roots of black metal. Taking USBM at a purely sonic level, it's obvious that it owes a huge debt to the Swedes and the Norwegians. It's pretty undeniable.

Wrath, Averse Sefira: I've been active in the underground for twenty years, and as far as I know there were virtually no American black metal bands before the Norwegian Incursion. Up until then, a majority of American acts were death metal, so while there are a lot of people who are desperate to deny that USBM owes most of its roots to Norway, it is pretty hard to prove otherwise.

Tyler Davis, Ajna Offensive: My first interests in BM were Darkthrone and Beherit -- two names mentioned in the *Kerrang!* article when Varg killed Euronymous.

Aesop Dekker, Ludicra/Agalloch: Around 1995 I was dumpster diving in San Francisco and I scored a copy of *Under a Funeral Moon* and I was set on my course. I had the same feeling I had when I discovered punk, like here's something totally alien and new, very exciting.

Andee, Aquarius Records/tUMULt: We had a cool co-op punk rock record store here in San Francisco called the Epicenter Zone, and one of the women who worked there was this insanely beautiful, statuesque, crusty punk girl with long multicolored dreads and spikes and leather and she was just like a total metal-crust pin-up. She was really into black metal, and started ordering more metal for the shop -- which I think ruffled some punk-rock feathers -- and one day she insisted I buy *In the Nightside Eclipse* and the very first cradle of Filth (still a fucking awesome record) and I was immediately hooked. To be honest, I would have probably bought anything she told me to, so good thing she had good taste.

Josh, Velvet Cacoon: I don't think anyone expected that a country as superficial as the U.S. could produce black metal that could tap into that weird obscurity that rests at the heart of this music.

He Who Crushes Teeth, Bone Awl: If you listen to the music, I think you can hear discernable qualities of American life. The stance is humble and masculine. It's a strong walk rather than elegant flight. There are no illusions of super powers or spiritual secrets. Life is enough of an explanation, like in transcendentalist writings, we don't need symbols or grandiose concepts to address the magic in life . . . Life and Death are adequate. The plain terms are adequate in expressing everything. Americans always take in pride in being focused, potent, and straightforward. The simplification of terms is our strongest American quality.

Tyler Davis, Ajna Offensive: I like some bands from the U.S. but never would have conceived of hording them altogether under some catchy, marketable little moniker like USBM. It implies a sense of unity, which I cannot see manifesting in the States on any comprehensible scale.

Imperial, Krieg: The whole idea of putting something in a category seems to be useful only in archiving. Obviously being from America and performing black metal would put any of us into the USBM category, but I don't see it as a subgenre, style or even any sort of outlined community really. It's just geography, or a way for someone who doesn't have anything to say with their music to try to relate to others that do.

Bestial Devotion, Negative Plane: I don't know, all that scene shit resembles an absurd club consisting of teenagers that never grew up in my eyes . . . Do they hold monthly meetings to discuss the further plans of "TEAM USBM"?

He Who Crushes Teeth, Bone Awl: USBM. United States Black Metal. What's not to like about it? Seems pretty self-explanatory. Seems like people are willing to go to great lengths to coin horrible sub genres. At least it's not "New Weird America" or "Forest Folk." Black Metal from the USA, sure, it works great.

W. Obscurum, Cult Of Daath: The U.S. scene is hard to generalize, especially these days. And there are some great minds among the trash, but on the rare occasion that I go to a show it seems to be brimming with hillbillies, leftist fags, and other assorted lowlifes. Maybe that was always the case.

Wrnlrd: I see people in the hallway and they seem as capable of black metal as I am. A few of them have appeared on my recordings without their knowledge, talking, crying, fucking, cursing through the walls . . . and some of them are children. So from my point of view "the scene is thriving."

Ancestors: Since people's entire lives are lies they need more lies to support their delusions. Scenes are all too happy to provide this infrastructure and attract other fellow deadbeats just like themselves. Scenes are breeding grounds for affectation and disease, soapboxes for those yearning to be defined as clichés. Nothing attracts more losers than a message.

He Who Crushes Teeth, Bone Awl: I think the first band to make a uniquely American statement in Black Metal was Grand Belial's Key. They use the same method as the Europeans in not just bending Death Metal a little bit but really making that leap, playing music that is rooted in the history of the country. Even though their music falls nicely into Black Metal as category, when I listen to *Mocking the Philanthropist* I hear American folk music, I hear the racial tension of the south, I hear hot American climates and landscapes. I hear the civil war. They did a fitting job including the surrounding culture into the sound, which most American bands completely fail to do.

Wrnlrd: Artistically, racist ideology certainly has a legitimate place in black metal, where frustrated people commonly act out fantasies of unrestrained hatred and power. I find no problems with a band using Nazi symbols or racist imagery to contextualize their music; I just don't usually find it to be done in a deeply interesting or original way. I personally take any band much more seriously when their approach to their own ideas is working on more than one level. Its possible to be blunt and nuanced, poetic and political at the same time. I think this complexity of viewpoint is what opens the door for music to be really rewarding for the listener, who can then find multiple ways to interpret what's going on for himself. This goes for NSBM too. Hypothetically, I do have a problem with the idea of giving my money to people who, I might reasonably assume, may use that money to fund violent attacks on other people. But I still pay taxes to the Federal Government. Life is made up of these subtle erosions of one's soul . . . until death. If I have to add "shopping for black metal CDs" to the list of moral dilemmas I encounter on a daily basis, it will be found somewhere at the bottom.

Blaash, Bahimron: The US has only been a country for about 225 years – we don't have the ancestry, and some places here don't have the majesty of nature – not to mention our (proposed) obsession on materialism and that we are all plastic and soulless consumers bent on working to buy stuff to buy a house to buy more stuff to work etc, etc. The extreme acts of the Nordic scene (murder, church burning) were also extremely fascinating and have never been topped by anyone within this "scene."

However, I would like to point out that this is where I actually prefer some of the more nihilistic leanings of USBM – the fact that we are covered in drugs, alcohol, a consumerism lifestyle, indeed – but is that not the work of the devil? We become soulless to a point – a hollow meandering consumer who thinks they are xtian until theyre rapin' their daughter one day . . . School shootings, mass murder, serial killers, suicide – all of the "real subjects" – not Viking heritage or killing the "Christians" in lyrics – I'm talkin' about real live church shootings, mass murder, warfare, forced prostitution, etc – it all happens here in the good ol' USA – we have had many, many more church burnings, it's called 'hatin' niggaz' here and is performed by the extreme right, and you go to j*ail* for it here, for many, many years, where if not careful, you learn to take it up the arse very badly.

D., Vrolok: Simply stated, I have absolutely no interest in politics or society. My physical existence is spent preparing for my astral existence (through the gathering of knowledge and experience), with everything else being rather trivial and more or less a way for me to pass time.

Dagon, Inquisition: Here in the United States you cannot play with fire like the early Norwegian scene. With terrorist threats all the time, the least you want to do in the name of black metal is become one right now. This is Satanic music, and that is how it must remain. If you want cheap fame, go kill yourself.

Aeesop Dekker, Ludicra/Agalloh: Believe me when I say there are bands and individuals who seek to bring about this sort of soap opera drama to the U.S. "scene." Bands that make empty threats and attempt to ignite feuds based on who is "true" and "worthy."I forget the name of the band from L.A. who had a member quit and become a born-again Christian, then the remaining members firebombed the rehab clinic he was an inpatient in. These sort of actions make for interesting news stories, but don't really say much about the individuals and the art they create.

He Who Crushes Teeth, Bone Awl: Europeans did a better job of mastering reality, but their psychology and actions can be destroyed just like anything else. It doesn't make them real . . . Black metal is the fiery combustion of a romantic ideal. I think the Europeans succeeded in becoming characters larger than themselves, and that's one of my worst fears: That I will somehow create a character that lives my own life without me.

Jordan, Wrath Of The Weak: In some respects, it seems like USBM has taken the destructive side of black metal and turned it against itself, so instead of church burnings and murders it manifests itself in the hatred and self-loathing that's present in a lot of the acts which get labeled as suicidal/depressive/etc. I suppose you could take that as a reaction of sorts against our current habit of ignoring and/or medicating away any mood that isn't neutral or somewhat positive.

Josh, Velvet Cacoon: True Satanism is wealth, wealth is psychedelic, and everything that occurs occurs as a dream.

Andee, Aquarius Records/tUMULt: Most black metal musicians did not grow up listening to black metal. Many might not have listened to metal at all. And you can hear that in the music: Elements of doom, psych, stoner rock, post rock. Black metal guys who are my age, which is a lot of them, were into Slint way before they were into black metal, and were listening to Drive Like Jehu and Unwound before they had ever heard Mayhem or Immortal. That stuff informs everything they do. Even when they're playing some part that is total Darkthrone worship, often those years of listening to other music seeps in and turns it into something new.

Imperial, Krieg: We were one of the first geographical groups to really tie in non black metal inspiration, like my covers of The Velvet Underground/The Stooges, etc, Leviathan/Lurker Of Chalice's Joy Division and Black Flag influences and covers, Nachtmystium's interest in psychedelics and more blues-based ideas, etc.

Dagon, Inquisition: We like it filthy. We don't want perfection. We don't want huge productions. We are doing what Europeans stopped doing ten years ago, which is making black metal without following the standards.

Blaash, Bahimiron: USBM incorporates more "brutality" I think then some European acts—ignoring the obvious stalwart murderers like Immortal, Marduk, or after them Dark Funeral . . .

Josh, Velvet Cacoon: Black metal is a drug of power, a study of the self, a warm and resinous Satanism. I see European black metal as being far more rooted in national romanticism and lore, whereas a good deal of USBM seems to exist more in the realm of fantasy, with lots of themes about space, alternate realities, physical powers.

Andee, Aquarius Records/tUMULt: It seems like the USBM scene has really embraced the personal nature of BM, the dark shadow of the soul, depression and sorrow, death and loss and longing.

He Who Crushes Teeth, Bone Awl: If you look at tendencies of bands in the US vs. Europe, you will find a trend towards individualism where as in Europe there is a stronger adherence to traditions. Of course there is the history of rugged individualism throughout American history, and in USBM history it's the same. I think really we look to Europe as the mother country of the genre and we look to it for acceptance and rebel against it simultaneously. I think the same theme of orphanization that has existed in American culture distinguishes USBM.

Imperial, Krieg: What I do see as something typically American (to which much outside of the US and unfortunately only a small portion within the country would agree) is the pseudo idea of American superiority to outside art, culture and music. This is why you see so many bands doing the paint by numbers sort of thing, regurgitating what's already been done yet thinking it's their own. As Americans we have a strong artistic and literary heritage, especially post WWII from the Beat movement, Warhol's idea of Popism, LaMonte Young's musical experiences etc but we don't draw on it, we just keep pushing out McBlackmetal.

Wrnlrd: I expect USBM inherits the fundamental American narrative of rebellion against European tyranny. All the elements of European metal that have been refined and perfected over the years are probably subject to that American mixture of reverence and contempt. The concept of the one-man-band has always flourished here, long before black metal, and I think this is quintessentially American. Obviously there are a lot of one-man black metal bands in Europe and many have produced essential, genre defining works. But also the idea of community seems to have resonated in Europe much more than in America -- this idea of connecting to the past and the spirits of one's ancestors. Viking metal, war themes. In the US I think it's the idea of the individual that resonates more powerfully, the strong individual with his own agenda: The pioneer, the entrepreneur, the lone gunman.

He Who Crushes Teeth, Bone Awl: You might come across American Black Metal and see a greater tendency to humanize the terms, which may seem somewhat contradictory. But I think an unknown goal in American Black Metal is to level the vocabulary and draw attention to the fact that nothing is outside of humanity. All of the evil, all of the monsters and demons, Satan are all within this scope and we can address the topics on these terms.

Imperial, Krieg: All of my work is based on my own deteriorating sense of reality, metal illness, fetish and natural ruin.

Ancestors: Black metal can only thrive on its own destruction. The longer a band stays functional, the more they come to symbolize life and development. Black metal must exist to destroy itself. Those few that I hold in high regard will hopefully kill themselves soon.

He Who Crushes Teeth, Bone Awl: It is about sacred rhythms. Underground rhythms. It is about simple meditation, one turn, the counter-thought and walking forward. The steady pace gives the movement its transparency. I don't see our music as aggressive; I see it as a contemplation of your own heartbeat. The heart never stops; it never stops until you're dead. It is never not drenched in blood. It is the most violent rhythm you can think of. When a body becomes so big it needs a heart, this is when music becomes real. Bone Awl's ideas of ascension are very humble, we obviously don't go too high, and don't have the same powers of flight like many European bands do. We work under a sun and we barely look up. We just know that life will one day end and about this we have a lot of questions.

Josh, Velvet Cacoon: USBM wasn't even respectable until the West Coast groups starting doing really innovative things with dissonance and oversaturated distortions a few years back. Until then you mostly had these beer-and-party metal bands from the East coast who had no real voice to their music, they were lackadaisically going through the motions. The east coast stuff was really incoherent and unconvincing, it offered nothing and went nowhere. There was no direction and it seemed like they were playing black metal because it was the alternative to being just a fan. Have you ever heard Kult ov Azazel or any of those types of east coast groups? Everything from the music to the lyrics, song titles and artwork screams "generic." I don't know how these guys get out of bed each morning. Plus, they lack personality. I know some people scoff at that notion in black metal but it does count for something. Could you imagine The Beatles without the personality of Lennon, or Pink Floyd without the personality of Syd? Personality behind the music is like an author's tone to his story . . .

He Who Crushes Teeth, Bone Awl: Anything good in American black metal is happening on the West Coast.... There is more culture in California. More global influence. More computers. Less McDonald's. More Starbucks. More Mexicans. More People. More numbers. Less women. More gay people. More cars. More traffic. More violence. More romance. More life in general. An abundance of living things.

Aesop Dekker, Ludicra/Agalloch: Xasthur always sounded French to me.

Killusion, The Howling Wind: I must admit the only Californian black metal I like is Leviathan.

He Who Crushes Teeth, Bone Awl: If you look at a band like Ashdautas you can pick out a lot of American qualities and Los Angeles' spirit. L.A. is large city. They're really dealing with the dismal satanic way of life in Los Angeles. The band is traditional and intuitive, terrestrial but they always have their eyes on the poisonous stars. There is a lot of space down there. You can find yourself on the edges facing the wideness of the night sky or you can end up being dwarfed again by huge buildings and seas of automobiles. There is enough depravity to draw from and the struggle of survival is so apparent that it is at once disillusioning and humbling. In their music you hear the varied landscapes, the huge "emotional switches", the dwarfing space, and the themes are usually grounded in focusing on human suffering rather than esoteric terms or abstract mythology.

Ancestors: The reality is things are happening everywhere, all around us, in secrecy.

Imperial, Krieg: If you read the American section of *Lords of Chaos* there isn't even much if any black metal mentioned. I've often thought a retrospective on US black metal like Ian Glasper's trilogy on English punk would be interesting, but what would it say? Most of the older generation have moved on, disappeared or just don't have anything to say outside of their own musical endeavors. We've all had interesting stories and experiences happen to us but outside of a dozen or so people from close to two decades there's just not much tabloid material in there and thus it wouldn't be interesting for the common person to read. And that just might be the beauty of it.

UMESH, Brown Jenkins: All it would take would be half a dozen ambitious writers in America and the U.S. black metal scene would have its own sordid narrative to struggle with. These are creations of the press, of course. If you think about it, the heart of the Norwegian narrative, for example, is a story with a black hole at the middle of it—no one really knows what happened the night Euronymous was murdered except Varg Vikernes. The other person involved is dead. Varg has told different stories about what happened over the years—does he even really remember? So even at the very center of an attempt to apply meaning and a grand, overarching story to the history of the Norwegian black metal scene, there is a wall beyond which no one can penetrate. It's meaningless. People can make whatever they want of it.

Wrnlrd: I see ghosts of American music everywhere. I hear Dock Boggs in black metal, the droning banjo, voice like an earthquake. I hear Blind Lemon pounding his feet on the floor, and I know he is my cousin. I find black metal in traffic noise. Whether the streets are German or Japanese. I think the essence of black metal is something that goes beyond geography and stylistic tradition, even beyond music.

PLAYING WOLVES AND RED RIDING HOODS IN BLACK METAL
Aspasia Stephanou

In the foggy embraces of maternal woods, where wolves and red riding hoods are lost and found, where strange becomings take place, at night, you can hear howls, growls, and grunts. Inarticulate words create gothic soundscapes of abject horror and ritualistic transgression. The limits between animal and human are crossed again and again in an uncanny repetition that respects no historical configuration of identity. Who is the lonely being that utters discordant, pre-linguistic cries amidst a chaotic symphony of sounds?

Wolves[1]

---

[1] The etymology of the word wolf according to the OED is: Com. Teut. and Indo-European: OE. wulf = OFris. wolf, OS., MLG. wulf, MDu. wolf, wulf (Du. wolf), OHG., MHG., G. wolf, ON. ulfr (Sw. ulf, Da. ulv), Goth. wulfs:- OTeut. *wulfaz. Feminine formations in Germanic are OE. wylf, OHG. wulpa (MHG. wülpe), ON. ylgr. Some definitions of the word from the OED: 1.a. A somewhat large canine animal (Canis lupus) found in Europe, Asia, and N. America, hunting in packs, and noted for its fierceness and rapacity. Also applied, with or without defining word, to various other species of Canis resembling or allied to this: see also PRAIRIE-wolf, TIMBER-wolf. b. In comparisons, with allusion to the fierceness or rapacity of the beast; often in contrast with the meekness of the sheep or lamb. 2. a. A person or being having the character of a wolf; one of a cruel, ferocious, or rapacious disposition. In early use applied esp. to the

I'm the Wolf incarnated as man. (Kadenzza)

> One beast and only one howls in the woods by night . . . At night, the eyes of wolves shine like candle flames, yellowish, reddish, but that is because the pupils of their eyes fatten on darkness and catch the light from your lantern to flash it back to you-red for danger; . . . But those eyes are all you will be able to glimpse of the forest assassins as they cluster invisibly round your smell of meat as you go through the wood unwisely late. They will be like shadows, they will be like wraiths, grey members of a congregation of nightmare; hark! His long, wavering howl . . . an aria of fear made audible. The wolfsong is the sound of the rending you will suffer, in itself a murdering. (Carter, 212)

In Black Metal the symbol of the wolf and the becoming-animal[2] of Deleuze and Guattari are metamorphosed into gothic

---

Devil or his agents (wolf of hell); later most freq., in allusion to certain biblical passages (e.g. Matt. vii. 15, Acts xx. 29), to enemies or persecutors attacking the 'flocks' of the faithful. b. slang. (a) A sexually aggressive male; a would-be seducer of women; (b) orig. U.S., a male homosexual seducer or one who adopts an active role with a partner. 3. Mus. a. 'The harsh howling sound of certain chords on keyed instruments, particularly the organ, when tuned by any form of unequal temperament' (Grove's Dict. Mus.); a chord or interval characterized by such a sound. After G. wolf (Arnolt Schlick, Spiegel der Orgelmacher, 1511).

[2] In *A Thousand Plateaus* Gilles Deleuze and Félix Guattari introduce the concept of "becoming-animal" which refers to the subject's movement from a stable position, from identity to a nomadic, anarchic existence. Deleuze and Guattari invoke gothic monsters such as

monsters multiplying and infecting with their contagious proliferations the dark of night. In Angela Carter's story wolves are assassins and the wolfsong is a murdering. Black metal glorifies the becoming-werewolf and werewolf nomadism characterised by aggression, speed and violence. The lycanthropic entities that are conjured up in black metal's lyrics along with the becoming-animal of the voice, demand from the listener a certain kind of response. Between a state of orgasmic pleasure and jouissance emanating from the performative space of radical otherness, and the horrors of hollowing up the body and transgressing its boundaries through the speed of sound, black metal is a monstrous desiring machine. From Pest's album *Hail the Black Metal Wolves of Belial* (2003) and the song "Possessed Wolves' Howling", rendered through the ferocious vocal chords of Satanic Tyrant Werwolf[8] aka Nazgul, to Lycanthropy's Spell and their songs "Werwolf" and "The Wolf Lord" and Black Funeral's "Der Werewolf" the trope of the wolf or werewolf seeks to destroy subjectivity. It enjoins a bestial annihilation of being and loss of humanity in order to expand the self into a creative multiplicity of wolves. Black metal is becoming wolf, embracing carnal desires, animal

---

vampires and werewolves whose transformation and contagious proliferation exemplifies the metamorphosis and the becoming-animal of the subject.

[3] Other Black Metal musicians have adopted new names to describe their becomings-wolf. Burzum's Kristian Vikernes has changed his name into Varg which means wolf. Darkthrone's Leif Nagell is known as Fenriz. Fenrir or Fenris is the name of the Nordic monstrous wolf, the son of the god Loki and Angerboda. Ulver is the name of a BM band from Norway whose lyrical themes are those of lycanthropy and fairy tales among others. Ulv means wolf in Norwegian and ulver is the plural form of the word.

transformations and violent instincts. Songs such as "Wolves Guard my Coffin" (Behemoth), "A Dream of Wolves in the Snow" (Cradle of Filth), "Werewolf, Semen and Blood" (Beherit), "The Burning Eyes of the Werewolf", "Legion Werewolf"(Satanic Warmaster), "Werewolf" (Temnozor), Gehennas's (Norway) "Werewolf" and "I Become a Werewolf Always" (Blackthrone) are fascinated with unnatural participations and wolfing (Deleuze and Guattari, 264). The black metal band becomes a pack of wolves effectuating continuous change. The anti-oedipal becomings of the sorcerers of black metal infect the listener, causing him or her to join into unholy alliances with the pack. In Black Funeral's "Der Werewolf" the lycanthropic contagion traverses body and soul:

> The lycanthropic strain engulfs my psyche and I feel electric alive . . .
> Holding the tetrahedron, the chant is called,
> Fenris is awakened . . . my eyes reflect red,
> Hungering, I walk the dense forestas the light of the fullmoon darkens the earth . . .
> And as I watch and feel the ghost rise . . . the energy builds,
> he acasual life envelops my being, to go into the world,
> To claw and devour the weak and fearful, beholden, upon a mountain . . .
> The purple lightning forms a sigil . . .
> Luna descends, the pleasures of flesh are mine!

The man becoming wolf calls forth the Fenris of the *Edda*, Norse mythology's monstrous wolf who swallows up Little Red Riding Hood, the leader of the pack, and as he forms an alliance with him, his being is transformed, and the primitive forces repressed by the Law are unleashed under the moon. The becoming-animal detests organization and desires anarchy: "to claw and devour" is the modus operandi of the wolfman. In a similar way, Satanic Warmaster celebrate "wolfish songs of fight, desecration and triumph" in the song "Legion Werewolf" calling for the "Satanic war legions" of werewolves to kill the "profaned remnants of the Christian god". However, for all its promise of revolutionary, liberatory becomings, black metal never arrives at a world of pure intensities. Black metal's wolves always refer to the past, and here Black Funeral refer to Norse mythology's symbols. There is a movement towards an original past, a desire to unearth the father signifier that incarcerates and forecloses the limitless powers of the wolf. At the same time the emphatic repetition of the violent attacks on the Christian god and His followers ironically undermines the force of black metal's transgressive agenda. The symbolic dismantling of law and religion leads to an equal loss of force in the transgressive act itself.

Wolves scream in thrilled terror or mournful tones, calling forth their evil father. A living incarnation of Satan has taken the place of a dead God. But the original father needs to be brought back and recomposed repeatedly for the transgressive act to have meaning. Logos demands to be there first, in order that Chaos may later renounce it, for the wolf to commit its prohibited crimes. Without a paternal figure transgression becomes a fruitless act, an empty simulation of repetition. And this is where black metal's contradictions take place. The thirst for annihilation, the violent transgression of limits, the disruption and the illicit crossing of boundaries are only manifested and secured with the presence of the phallus. The Christian father haunts black metal, the way King Hamlet's ghost haunts Denmark. In an interpretation of the fairy tale of red riding hood, the girl carrying bread and wine to her grandmother embodies Christ who comes to humans in flesh and blood, bread and wine. Black metal's transgressions are the spectral fruits of the Garden of Eden. Dislocation of proper categories such as melody, speech, language, and meaning is the negative event of their recognition as categories and their acceptance.

For Paul Virilio, the "high priest of speed", speed exemplifies our modern technological condition. Everything is accelerated into a dehumanising prison for the modern subject. While black metal desires and mourns for a primordial original past, a utopian vision of nature and ancestral purity that never were, it does so through the speeding up of metallic war machines. The fast paced rhythms that as Ronald Bogue asserts, "produce sonic analogues of the sounds, rhythm and patterns of the modern technological lifeworld" (40) are coupled with lyrics evoking pastoral, idyllic and oneiric paradisiacal landscapes. Again, black metal's contradictory manifestation of opposing forces takes place. The annihilation of melody and the repetition of raw sounds of the same fast tempo reflect the condition of modernity's mechanical reproductive experience, the simulation of simulations, the emptiness of the sign, the disenfranchised being's uniform activities. While the listener is frozen into a space of non-response-how am I to dance or move when the speed of music confuses body and mind?- this blank topos violently breaks down with the singer's high-pitched screeches re-establishing that the double negativity of unnatural voice and metallic noise is an affirmation of being here and now.

Black metal's attack on the despotic father through the unproductive expenditure of intense flows reaffirms the master signifier's authority. Despite the seemingly unorganised tempo and the revolutionary anti-melodic uses of instruments and voice, black metal is perfectly obedient to the dialectic of control and the power of order and the Law. As Keith Kahn Harris argues, "extreme metal reduces musical freedom..., until it appears only in order that it can be controlled. Extreme metal often sounds close to being a formless noise, but backs away from doing so at the last moment" (34). This is also obvious in the ways guitar solos or melody associated with the feminine body and the abject are controlled. This kind of control of the presence and absence of the feminine resemble the child's game with the cotton reel. Freud's discussion in *Beyond the Pleasure Principle* about the child's *fort-da* game and the repetition of the disappearance and appearance of the object are a useful way to reflect on the tensions arising in the deterritorializations and reterritorializations occurring in black metal compositions. Whether following Freud's reading of the game as a substitute for the absence of the mother or Lacan's reading of the game as the child's entrance into the symbolic and signification, the appearance and disappearance of the cotton reel recalls the similar ways that the abject is controlled in black metal. Black metal musicians repeat this game of absence of melody and its appearance in order to affirm masculinity and domination over the abject musical forms such as melody. Specifically in Lacan's understanding of the game, the cotton reel is associated with the *petit a*. This reel, Lacan says, "is not the mother reduced to a little ball by some magical game worthy of Jivaros – it is a small part of the subject that detaches itself from him while still remaining his, still retained" (62). The object a is a hole, a daemonic space of nothing in which a "persisting tension", the vacillating rhythm of life and death, creation and destruction take place. Between the pleasure principle and the death drive or "mother drive", between moving forwards and back, black metal's vacillating rhythms trigger the desire to create something new. As Lacan reminds us, there is no *fort* without Dasein, without presence. But "no subject can grasp this radical articulation" which is an exercise referring to an alienation and not to a mastery. (239).

In the "Futurist Manifesto" (1909), Marinetti proclaimed that "Beauty exists only in struggle. There is no masterpiece that has not an aggressive character. Poetry must be a violent assault on the forces of the unknown, to force them to bow before man." Between the feminine forces and the aggressive violence of masculine agency black metal narrates dark fairy tales about wolves and red riding hoods. In Kadenzza's album *The Second Renaissance* (2005) songs based on the story of little red riding hood manifest the wolf's masculine authority over the maternal and feminine. "In the Woods" red riding hood creeps through a hole in the door only to find the wolf offering her the flesh of her dead mother as food. It seems that both the wolf and red riding hood have transgressed into the mother's house, the womb in the forest. In "The Wolfoid" the wolf incarnated as man unleashes his violent instincts through aggressive vocals and fast, repetitive, symphonic parts that deliver his nightmarish visions of devouring the mother and red riding hood. It is the "sinful nectar" dripping from red riding hood's "nasty lips" that arouses the beast. Unable to make any choices red riding hood will have to drink the blood and eat the flesh of her mother, until finally the wolf will consume her body. Here Kadenzza play with the oral tradition of this fairy tale before Perault's version which included the cannibalistic act of eating the grandmother and presented red riding hood as a slut who would eat the flesh and drink the blood of her grandmother. Wolves are the evil seducers whose ferocious instincts drive them in the consummation of their female victims. The threat of female sexuality, the threat of the red hood, the colour of sacrifices, the colour of the girl's menses (Carter, 219) need to be destroyed by the wolf.

Red Riding Hoods

Entering the *Satanic Church of the Dead* on virtual space, Satanic Corpse's Belita Adair hails Satan dressed in a red hood. According to Erich Fromm the cap of red velvet is a symbol for menstruation, of abject matter (Dundes, 211). Are red riding hoods a destabilizing force in the wolf-dominated Black metal?

If wolves devour the female in a cannibalistic sexual act that simulates the power of women to bear children, then how do red riding hoods respond? In Astarte's song "Thorns Of Charon - Part I (Astarte's Call)" wolves become the servants of Astarte, the goddess of fertility, sexuality and war. The empty, male bodies locked in Astarte's cages of steel will be resurrected only when the goddess summons their souls. Reclaiming the realm of female desire, female black metal bands challenge the patriarchal structures of black metal. Rosolato writes that "music finds its roots and its nostalgia in [this] original atmosphere, which might be called a sonorous womb, a murmuring house, or music of the spheres" (qtd. in Shepherd and Wicke, p.86). The relation of music to the sound of the mother's voice for the newborn infant entails however both pleasure and trauma. The mother's voice being associated with the abject, what Kristeva names as the "jettisoned object" which is "radically excluded and draws me toward the place where meaning collapses" (2) brings music closer to the pre-symbolic level. This regression takes the subject to the place of the semiotic chora, of the maternal. If wolves howl, then red riding hoods can scream non-linguistic forms attacking the symbolic order. While wolves control and violate female presence in the lyrics, melody and the use of high-pitched vocals, female black metal bands delight in the abject through jouissance. Black metal bands violently mourn for the loss of an object that has already been lost. The ego, Kristeva reminds us, through the abject, goes back to the abominable limits from which has already broken away from. Abjection is "an alchemy that transforms death drive into a start of life, of new significance" (15). Gallhammer with guttural screams desire the death of the father in "Tomurai" and Astarte announce the war machine of the mother Astarte. From Keat's "Ode on Melancholy" to the ecstasies of metallic desiring machines, Melencolia Estatica, the project of the mysterious Climaxia, gives free rein to both aggression and romantic intensity. The sexual difference that these female black metal bands try to incorporate into black metal's structures, a rewriting of female desire into the codes of music is a challenging creative power that destroys the "silence" assigned to them by the phallus. But in such a nihilistic place, black metal's red riding hoods are forced to join with the wolves (Demonic Christ), disappear behind masks (Melencolia Estatica), or oversexualize themselves (Astarte). In Angela Carter's "The Company of Wolves" red riding hood is becoming woman and chooses to sleep with the tender wolf. However, difference and anarchic becomings, as Hal Foster warns, "are also privileged terms of advanced capitalism" and that "difference is an object of consumption too" (212). For female black metal bands or women in black metal bands becoming-woman needs to be achieved through a process of self-assertion and then of transformation, as Braidotti argues (60). This primary narcissism, as opposed to the secondary narcissism of vanity and the love of appearances that leads to objectification, is necessary for women to accomplish metamorphoses. If female black metal bands manipulate the qualities that patriarchy has endowed them with through the use of sexuality in their performances, the language of nihilism or the repetition of black metal's masculine discourses, then the perpetuation of the similar will persist and their presence will forever be silenced. Black metal is a strange place to be. In a genre in which misanthropy is related to misogyny and in which male authority mostly ignores the feminine presence, black metal's red riding hoods whether they choose, as the fairy tale says, the path of needles or the path of pins, they must still fight both the father and the wolves to survive in the woods.

Works Cited

Adair, Belita. *Satanic Church of the Dead.* Belita Adair, 2006-2009. Web. 12 Jan. 2009.
< http://www.sataniccorpse.com/satanicchurch.html>.

Bogue, Ronald. "Violence in Three Shades of Metal: Death, Doom and Black." *Deleuze's Way: Essays in Traverse Ethics and Aesthetics.* Hampshire and Vermont: Ashgate Publishing, 2007.

Braidotti, Rosi. *Metamorphoses: Towards a Materialist Theory of Becoming.* Cambridge: Polity, 2002.

Carter, Angela. "The Company of Wolves." *Burning Your Boats: Collected Stories.* Intro. Salman Rushdie. London: Vintage Books, 2006. 212-220.

Deleuze, Gilles and Félix Guattari. *A Thousand Plateaus: Capitalism and Schizophrenia*. 1987. Trans. Brian Massumi. London and New York: Continuum, 2004.

Dundes, Alan, ed. *Little Red Riding Hood: A Casebook*. Wisconsin and London: The University of Wisconsin Press, 1989.

Foster, Hal. *The Return of the Real: The Avant-Garde at the End of the Century*. Cambridge, Massachusetts: MIT Press, 1996.

Freud, Sigmund. "Beyond the Pleasure Principle." *The Standard Edition of the Complete Psychological Works of Sigmund Freud: Beyond the Pleasure Principle, Group Psychology and Other Works*. Vol. XVIII (1920-1922). London: The Hogarth P, 1955. 1-64.

Harris, Keith-Kahn. *Extreme Metal: Music and Culture on the Edge*. Oxford and New York: Berg, 2007.

Kristeva, Julia. *Powers of Horror*: An Essay on Abjection. Trans. Leon S. Roudiez. New York: Columbia U P, 1982.

Lacan, Jacques. *Four Fundamental Concepts of Psychoanalysis*. Ed. Jacques-Alain Miller. Trans. Alan Sheridan. London: The Hogarth P, 1977.

Marinetti, F. T. *The Futurist Manifesto* (1909). <http://www.cscs.umich.edu/ ~crshalizi/T4PM/ futurist-manifesto.html>

Shepherd, John, and Peter Wicke. *Music and Cultural Theory*. Cambridge: Polity P, 1997.

Discography

Astarte. "Thorns of Charon- Part I (Astarte's Call)." *Doomed Dark Years*. Black Lotus Records, 1998.

Behemoth. "Wolves Guard my Coffin." *Sventevith (Storming Near the Baltic)*. Pagan Records, 1995.

Beherit. "Werewolf, Semen and Blood." *Drawing Down the Moon*. Spinefarm Records, 1994.

Black Funeral. "Der Werewolf." *Empire of Blood*. Full Moon Productions, 1997.

Blackthrone. "I Become a Werewolf Always." *Panzerfaust Division Blackthrone*. Satanic, 2001. Demo.

Cradle of Filth. "A Dream of Wolves in the Snow." *The Principle of Evil Made Flesh*. Cacophonous Records, 1994.

Gallhammer. "Tomurai: May Our Father Die." *Gloomy Lights*. Goatsucker Records, 2004.

Gehenna. "Werewolf." *WW*. Moonfog Productions, 2005.

Kadenzza. "In the Woods." *The Second Renaissance*. Holy Records, 2005.

---. "Wolfoid." *The Second Renaissance*. Holy Records, 2005.

Lycanthropy's Spell. "The Wolf Lord." *Pagan Alliance*. Darkmare Productions, 2004.

---. "Werwolf." *Chaos, Death and Horror*. Darkmare Records, 2003.

Pest. "Possessed Wolves' Howling."*Hail the Black Metal Wolves of Belial*. BloodFireDeath/Vinland Winds, 2003.

Satanic Warmaster. "The Burning Eyes of the Werewolf." *Werewolf Hate Attack*. Guttural Records, 2007. EP.

---."Legion Werewolf." *Werewolf Hate Attack*. Guttural Records, 2007. EP.

Temnozor. "Werewolf." *Horizons* . . . Ascent Records, 2003.

GOATSTEPS BEHIND MY STEPS . . . : BLACK METAL AND RITUAL RENEWAL
Anthony Sciscione

Black metal, more so than most any genre of music, is concerned both sonically and thematically with thermal intensities. The blueprint for the modern sound strongly encodes resonances of its origins in the frigid Scandinavian North, and despite its southern passage through networks of geographic and cultural transformational influence it has retained a characteristic level of coldness as an immanent quality. However, one has to look no further than the cover of Immortal's "Diabolical Fullmoon Mysticism," old Bathory publicity photos or shirtless shots of Blasphemy in a Vancouver cemetery showmanly blowing fire skyward from a concentration of flame to note that heat is equally significant to the black metal aesthetic. "Freezing" atmospheres of, say, Judas Iscariot or Old Wainds easily give way to the "blazing," "burning," hell-fire clamor of bands like the German Katharsis, 1349, or Averse Sefira without any drastic alteration of formal principles, and the force that mediates between these thermal intensities is a sort of *conductive violence*, a constant and potent accident of atmosphere that has the quality of a heat-transference which works upon something and draws it toward a limit, one of either over-excitation or exhaustion. While intensities of hot and cold are thermodynamic polarities, at their outermost extremities they converge as peripheral markers of sensory tolerance that are contingent with an immediate threat of destabilization and breakdown which *must* be responded to, either by retreating and escaping to more hospitable and equilibrious grounds, or remaining and allowing oneself to be driven beyond all thresholds of tolerability, to the point where a fundamental change-of-state is inevitable. To have either force at one's disposal is to wield a power that menaces the stability of any system it may be set against. So in terms of their mutual capacity to provoke critical alterations of phase, fire and ice are kindred harbingers of conductive violence; to pervert a line of the great God-fearing English poet George Herbert, "what pole is not the zone, / Where all things burn [?]" (*The Flower* ll. 32-3). Black metal's intimate rapport with limits and intense states is precisely what necessitates its banishment to the periphery of the social, which relies on temperateness and stability to inform its standards of operation. Like any such system, it cannot abide the integration of radically unstable forces without rupturing or otherwise suffering a degradation of its structural integrity. "The scent of your weakness excites this metal," screeches Leviathan in "Mine Molten Armor," "I will meet you with war." The intent of this paper is to explore in what capacities and to what extent black metal, insofar as it holds to its identity as a peripheral, adversarial force, conceives of the destruction it threatens as productive of new orders of being in terms of both self and cosmos. In short, what states are beyond its thresholds?

A slideshow of tropic black metal imagery clicks away; shots of snow-weighted pine forests, static mountain light crosswhipped grey with ice fog, tundra expanses, a *paysage d'hiver* of stagnated lakes and blizzard burials. The recession, into darkness, of a hooded figure lapsing from presence into scowling and ascetic withdrawal, into an outflow of repellent frequencies that create distance by overtaking and immobilizing, tacitly coaxing one into a space of self-seclusion that resists the self-exposing conditions of the world-space by freezing it back, sonically whiting it out. Such grim withdrawal gathers itself into a liminal, polar space to nurse a blackening frost, a clandestine blaze which builds qualitatively against the world and threatens at any moment to seize up and overtake it. Immortal's "Antarctica" imagines that continent spreading its thermal influence over the globe: "Behind the gates and mighty portals / Of the arctic polar circle / Builds the frozen layers of snow / A perfect platform to grow against the seasons / The snowbelts of Antarctica rise / With its dark polar winterstorms" (Immortal, "Antarctica"). For Immortal, the freezing of the world is not an end in itself, a glorification of stasis, but is rather creative insofar as it heralds the return of a mythic ancestral past where ice winds carried ancient Norsemen to battle in black skies. Conceptually, the existing world must be frozen back, stopped, because it presents itself as incongruous with the realization of the fantastic ideal. It is precisely in terms of this incongruity that Immortal's adversarial force is concentrated, as they in turn embrace the bellicose ideal and offer themselves as vessels or carriers of it. At the same time they connect a mystical ideal to this past: "North black hordes storm / Through invincible cyclones of frostwinds / I lift my hands / And join the ceremonial circle of one wind." Here, the movement of battle sanctifies an engulfing ice vortex that harmonizes the self with a center of polar energy. Another song envisions the effects of being driven to the threshold where identity is yielded to frost: "Frostbitten I became, forthwith to see, crystalized dimensions . . . You must come to me. There are nocturnal paths to follow" (Immortal, "Grim and Frostbitten Kingdoms"). Similarly, Emperor's "Ensorcelled by Khaos" dramatizes a submission to the overwhelming forces of lust and war which offer an escape from the "endless mazes" that entrap the seeker in his search for death: "Take me--Venus, Seduce me; Mars, Possess me; Tear my soul from sanity." In each case, being taken beyond a threshold by the conductive violence of a tactile intensity involves a new opening-up of the self and a restitution of identity on the basis of now belonging to that power and having become an expression of its potency.

In a similar vein, isolationist, misanthropic black metal draws the sources of its adversity to existence into itself, localizing in the individual the very forces of misery and dejection that make the world worth withdrawing from in the first place. The negative forces he internalizes become him, overcome him, and he lowers himself in submission to them so as to become an arbiter of their power. Still room; dust-scented darkness, thicker in corners; steel razor focalizing to pinpoint harshness rays of expiring exterior light; forearm veins taut and pulsing purple, networks of vitalistic entrapment: to quote Leviathan, "cut through deep / now set it free / cut through deep / from these depths /the gift and chalice / pain must be the course / I must have this / don the horns and the skull / pain is the path" (Leviathan, "He Whom Shadows Move Towards"). Rituals of excruciating pain, writes Victor Turner, have the effect of "rendering [the individual] down to a sort of human *prima materia*, divested of a specific form and reduced to a condition that...is without or beneath accepted forms of status" (Turner 170). Wrest's sonic paths of pain, however, most usually do not lead to any sort of regenerative empowerment, but rather reassert the primacy of the liminal state where the potential of a thing to integrally withstand violence is transgressed. At the end of possibly the most awesomely-titled song ever, "Fucking Your Ghost in Chains of Ice," Wrest invites the hearer to convene and assimilate with fellow suicided spirits in an torturous void of extinction over which "horrors" preside, instruments of degradation that, through various methods of constraining and frictional compression, perpetually remind one of the weakness and fragility of the human. When levelled at the cosmos as a whole, the conductive violence of his aesthetic is concerned with driving vitality to an icy stasis approaching absolute zero, to a point away from renewal and beyond redemption. We see this in the lyrics to "The Idiot Sun," which are rife with images of wastedness and exhaustion: "lifeless burnt-out sphere / now frozen to black /and ice is wept by the sun / stifled by crystal universe / arctic pitch black pyre / of this sky no more / lifeless burnt-out sphere / self destruction universe" (Leviathan, "Idiot Sun").

In Wrest's vision of cosmic cessation, fire is connected to vital, life-giving energy, and the extinguishment of the sun signals the terminal triumph of darkness and ice which are employed for their suggestion of anguish and pain alone. Conversely, we see in Averse Sefira's "Detonation" the transformative properties of fire employed for purposes of renewal: "Before reemergence / In a new radiance / The world must burn / In rebirth / Bear witness to this rise!" In a state of incineration the world is an intensity-in-transition, a system forced to a state of maximum agitation whereby it is conducted toward an open, purified state. This vision of cosmic destruction is expressed in purely material terms, and it displays conductive violence levelled not at being itself but at a particular orientation of being from which vital forces must be liberated so they may reform in new configurations. "All fetters melt away / Releasing the pulchritude / Of mastery / Obfuscated in the face / Of the moral / Blood flesh / Death earth / New life taken / Taking shape" (Averse Sefira,"Transitive Annihilation"). Likewise, in Altar of Perversion's "Wisdom of Evil," the speaker passes through the threshold of death in order to gain occult knowledge from Choronzon, the Dweller in the Abyss, pledging: "I will kill what I called myself / and wear your mark as my eye / And wear your horns as my crown / I return, goatsteps behind my steps . . . " He withdraws into a liminal space that exceeds the capacity for mortality to withstand it, and undergoes a sacrificial demise in order to open himself up as a habitat for and an expression of the power of the demon. But of him we can say what Bataille says of the sovereign, which is that he "doesn't die, for he dies only to be reborn. He is not a man in the individual sense of the word, but rather a *god*; he is essentially the embodiment of the one he is but is not. He is the same as the one he replaces; the one who replaces him is the same as he" (Bataille, "The Schema of Sovereignty," 319). This collapsing of identities is a matter of mutual empowerment in the sense that the demon is granted access to the open world, the realm from which death is kept in concealment, while the self is renewed by opening itself to the powers of death and centering the peripheral, or making standard a liminal state of being.

What these examples attest to is that renewal in black metal frequently involves a realization of things in excess of themselves, at or beyond the limit of their possible expressions. As voiced by the Polish act Mgła: "Beyond the border / On the other side of myself / In each drop of poison, in each strand of saliva / I am." The conductive violence that drives a system toward over-excitation or exhaustion is motivated by a dissatisfaction with medial states and a manifest lust for the intensity of transitions, of ceding or forcing a system to cede to a radical alterity that reconfigures identity by destroying and overtaking. Black metal's discourse of renewal is grounded upon its harnessing of polar energies in collusion with its antagonistic posturing against standard, non-intense social and ontological states. I will let a quote from Nightbringer's "Womb of Nyx" serve as a final illustration of this process of productive destruction: "And with a single word and the breath of flame, I bring forth the Dawn / Let the wary weep as slumber turns to death / Let the earth smolder and heave as the Golden Pillars rise (Nightbringer, "Womb of Nyx").

THREE QUESTIONS ON DEMONOLOGY
Eugene Thacker

The life of every individual, viewed as a whole and in general, and when only its most significant features are emphasized, is really a tragedy; but gone through in detail it has the character of a comedy.
—Arthur Schopenhauer

QUÆSTIO I – On the Meaning of the Word "Black" in Black Metal

ARTICULUS

Discussions of music genres often revolve around what does or doesn't constitute the essence of that genre. When disagreements arise, a common solution is simply to divide the genre into subgenres. Metal is no exception to this pattern, and there are more and more metal subgenres every day. Metal is no longer just heavy, it's also death, speed, grind, doom, funeral, and of course black. That said, while there is no shortage of discussion on metal as a music genre, there is less discussion on all the adjectives that make one subgenre distinct from another. What, for example, is the "black" in black metal? In its popular associations, black metal is called black for a wide range of reasons – its references to black magic, demons, witchcraft, lycanthropy, necromancy, the nature of evil, and all things dark and funereal. Black metal is black because it is – this is one argument at least – the most extreme form of metal, both in its attitude and in its musical form.

Of all these associations, there is one thing that sticks out, and that is the association of black metal to Satansim and the figure of the Devil. In fact, it would seem that this equation is the defining factor of black metal: *Black = Satanism*. Obviously this is a reduction, and we will undo it later on. To begin with, however, we have to keep in mind the complicated history of translation and terminology, as the term *satan* or *ha-satan* passes from the Hebrew Bible (where it designates an angelic divinity that tests one's faith) to the Koine Greek of the Septuagint, to the Latin Vulage of the Old Testament, before its apperance in the Gospels, where the figure of Satan is often depicted as a malefic figure poised against the monotheistic God, rather than against humanity per se. At different points in the long history of Christianity, the figure of Devil, as this universal antagonist of God and humanity, is given different names, Satan being only one of them, and it is with this figure with which the "black" is black metal may arguably be identified. Certainly black metal is neither the only metal subgenre, nor the only music genre generally, to have made this association. One can just as easily find it in the music of Robert Johnson or the *Carmina Burana* as one could in bands like Black Sabbath. But the degree to which Satanism constitutes a conceptual reference point for black metal is indeed striking.

For the moment, then, let us think about "black" as meaning Satanic. What does this imply conceptually? For one, if we take the Medieval and early Renaissance notion of Satan as a starting point, the equation black = Satanism is governed by a structure of opposition and inversion. Opposition defines the demonic as much as the divine; it is the "War in Heaven" described so vividly in *Revelations*, and dramatized in Milton's *Paradise Lost*. Opposition is also the structure that comes to define the Medieval Church against its foes, the role that the Church councils accord various activities, from witchcraft to necromancy, as threats to both religious law and religious political authority. This opposition, then, is as much political as it is theological, resulting in the infamous witch-hunts, persecutions, and trials of the early Renaissance. In its oppositional mode, the equation black = Satanic means "against God," "against the Sovereign," or even "against the divine."

Cover for Darkthrone's *Transylvanian Hunger* (Peaceville, 1994).

The image of Satanism takes on a different form by the 19th century, however. In a sense, one cannot really even talk about Satanism before this time, at least not as an organized counter-religion complete with its own rituals, texts, and symbols. What we would call Satanism before this time was, legally speaking, defined by the Church as heresy, and heresy is a particular kind of threat – it is not the threat of not believing at all, but the threat of believing in the "wrong" way. By contrast, 19th century Europe, following upon the religious challenges posed by

Romanticism, the Revolution, and the aesthetics of the gothic and decadent movements, developed something that more resembles modern Satanism. It is markedly different from the Medieval and early Renaissance versions as it is from its later-20th century incarnations (e.g. Antoine LaVey's Church of Satan). This more formalized, "poetic" Satanism operated not only by opposition, but by inversion, as demonstrated in Charles Baudelaire's then-scandalous poem "Les Litanies de Satan" (1857). This Satanism is ritually, as well as ideologically, opposed to the Church. In its 19th century context, it overlaps considerably with occultism, magic, and even off-shoots of spiritualism. A key aspect of this poetic Satanism is the infamous Black Mass, deliriously portrayed in Joris-Karl Huysmans' novel *Là-bas* (1891; tr. *Down There*) – which is purportedly based on a real Black Mass the author had attended. Every element of the Black Mass, from the blasphemous anti-prayer to the erotic desecration of the host, aims at an exact inversion of the Catholic High Mass.

If we take the "black" in black metal to mean Satanic, then see how this is emblematic of a conceptual structure of opposition (its Medieval, "heretical" variant) and inversion (its 19th century, "poetic" variant). In this association we also see a relation to the natural world and supernatural forces as the means through which opposition and inversion is effected. The "black" in this case is nearly like a technology, a dark technics. Black magic in particular is predicated on the ability of the sorcerer to utilize dark forces against light, one set of beliefs against another.

SED CONTRA

On the contrary, it is obvious to any listener of black metal that not all black metal bands ascribe to this equation of black =

Satanic. There are many black metal bands that take a non-Christian framework as their foundation, referencing everything from Norse mythology to the mysteries of ancient Egypt. We can take a different approach, then, and suggest another meaning to the word "black" in black metal, and that is: *Black = pagan*. We will undo this yet again, but for the time being let us think about this in contrast to the black = Satanism meaning.

To begin with, paganism denotes less a negative or reactive mode, than an entirely different, and ultimately pre-Christian outlook. Historically, the different forms of paganism overlap with the rise of Christianity as a dominant religious, juridical, and political force. Paganism, as a polytheistic – and sometimes pantheistic – viewpoint, stood in stark contrast to the doctrinal sovereignty of the Church. Because of this, forms of paganism were often inculcated within what the Church ambiguously called heresy. During the high Renaissance a wide range of activities, from alchemy to shamanism, were popularly associated with paganism. The ideas of Rosicrucianism, Freemasonry, Hermeticism, and, in the 19th century, theosophy and spiritualism, all claimed some connection to a pagan outlook. The ambit and scope of some of these movements is even more expansive than Christianity itself; the writings of Madame Blavatsky and Rudolph Steiner, for instance, are exemplary in their trans-cultural and trans-historical breadth. In books such as *Isis Unveiled* (1877) or *The Secret Doctrine* (1888), Blavatsky covers everything from archaic mystery cults to modern paranormal research, giving one the sort of global perspective found in anthropology classics such as James Frazer's *The Golden Bough* (1890).

Cover for Ulver's *Nattens Madrigal* (Century Media, 1997).

While these different forms of paganism sometimes overlap with the traditional Judeo-Christian outlook, they are more often than not marginalized, and, in some cases, driven underground into secret societies. Here we see one major difference from the prior association of "black" with Satanism. Whereas the latter operated through opposition and inversion, the former is related to the dominant framework of Christianity by exclusion and alterity. Whereas heresy was viewed by the Church primarily as in internal threat, with paganism one finds, in some cases, an entirely different framework – an external threat. The images are also different. Instead of demonic invocations and the Black Mass, there may be images of animistic nature, elemental and earth powers, astral lights and astral bodies, the metamorphoses of human and animal, human and plant, human and nature itself. In paganism one is always "on the side of" nature and its animistic forces. The magician is less one who uses nature as a tool, and more like a conduit for natural forces. Whereas in

Satanism one finds an attempt to instrumentalize the dark forces against light, in paganism magic is technology and vice-versa. Works like Eliphas Lévi's *Dogme et Rituel de la Haute Magie* (1855) read like a veritable how-to book of occult knowledge, theories, and practices. In contrast to the dark technics of Satanism, then, the dark magic of paganism.

RESPONSIO

We have, then, two possible meanings that the word "black" can have in phrases like black metal. These is black = Satanism and black = paganism. One has the structure of opposition and inversion, and other the structure of exclusion and alterity. Both are united, however, in what amounts to a human-oriented relation to nature and natural force – with Satanism we see a dark technics of dark vs. light forces, and with paganism we see a dark magic of being-on-the-side of nature itself. Despite their differences, both meanings of the term "black" point to one thing they have in common, and that is an anthropocentric view towards the world. The world is either there for us to use as a tool, or it is there inside us as a force for our benefit. Even as the various forms of paganism adopt an animistic or pantheistic view of the world, they also assert a means of knowing and utilizing the forces of that world; the self is at once united with the world and yet split from it. The human point of view seems to be a limit for thought in both of these meanings of "black" (Satanism and paganism).

Is there yet another alternative meaning of "black" beyond this? There is, but it is a difficult thought to think, and nearly impossible to know, though it does exist (actually it doesn't exist, though the thought of its not-existing does). As we noted, both the Satanic and pagan variants of the word "black" remain minimally committed to the perspective of the human, even as they posit forces in the world beyond all comprehension. The result is that these dark forces are in some way always "for us" as human beings (either as wielding darkness or "being on the side of" darkness). Whereas both the Satanic and pagan variants retain an anthropocentric thread, a third position, which we can call "cosmic," attempts to relinquish even this. There is only the anonymous, impersonal "in itself" of the world, indifferent to us as human beings, despite all we do to change, to shape, to improve and even to save the world. We could be even more specific and refer to this perspective not just as cosmic, but as a form of "Cosmic Pessimism." The view of Cosmic Pessimism is a strange mysticism of the world-without-us, a hermeticism of the abyss, a noumenal occultism. It is the difficult thought of the world as absolutely unhuman, and indifferent to the hopes, desires, and struggles of human individuals and groups. Its limit-thought is the idea of absolute nothingness, unconsciously represented in the many popular media images of nuclear war, natural disasters, global pandemics, and the cataclysmic effects of climate change. Certainly these are the images, or the specters, of Cosmic Pessimism, and different from the scientific, economic, and political realities and underlie them; but they are images deeply embedded in our psyche nonetheless. Beyond these specters there is the impossible thought of extinction, with not even a human subject to think the absence of all human subjects, with no thought to think the negation of all thought. Hence another possible meaning of the term "black": *Black = Cosmic Pessimism*.

Cosmic Pessimism has a genealogy that is more philosophical than theological. Its greatest – and most curmudgeonly – proponent was Arthur Schopenhauer, the misanthrope who rallied as much against philosophy itself as he did against doctrinal religion and the nationalist politics of his about a human pessimism (e.g. the all-too-human despair of an identity crisis or a lapse in faith), and more about the way in which thought in itself always devolves on its own limits, the hinge through which positive knowledge turns into negative knowledge. To find an equal to Schopenhauer, one would have to look not to philosophy but to writers of supernatural horror such as H.P. Lovecraft, whose stories evoke a sense of what he termed "cosmic outsideness" – the black tentacular voids that surround us and that stretch into the furthest "black seas of infinity." In summary, then, another meaning of the word "black" – not Satanism with its opposition/inversion and dark technics, not paganism with its exclusion/alterity and dark magic, but a Cosmic Pessimism, with its dark metaphysics of negation, nothingness, and the non-human.

On the surface, it would seem that black metal bands would fall into one of these three meanings of the word "black." For instance, old school Norwegian black metal would seem to fit the Satanic meaning of black, as evidenced by albums such as Darkthrone's *Transylvanian Hunger*, Emperor's *Wrath of the Tyrant*, Gorgoroth's *Pentagram*, and Mayhem's *De Mysteriis Dom Sathanas*. Likewise, it would seem that other black metal bands might fit the pagan meaning of black, as exhibited in Ulver's *Nattens Madrigal*, Ildjarn's *Forest Poetry*, Striborg's *Mysterious Semblance*, and Wolves in the Throne Room's *Diadem of Twelve Stars*. One could even suggest that some of the formal experiments in black metal, from the minimalism of Sunn O)))'s *Grimmrobe Demos* to the wall-of-noise in Wold's *Stratification* might offer musical equivalents of the Cosmic Pessimism meaning of the word black.

HIDEOUS GNOSIS

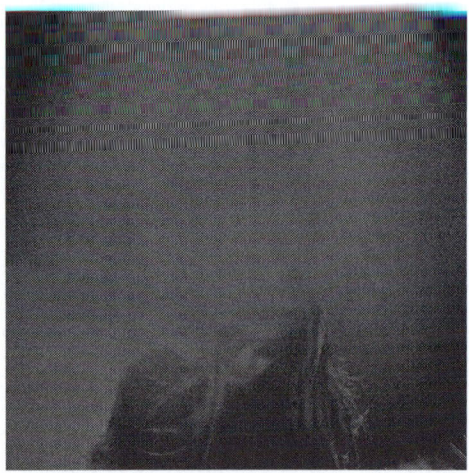

Cover for Keiji Haino's *So, Black is Myself* (alien8, 1997).

I would suggest, however, that this third kind of "black," that of Cosmic Pessimism, in actually implicit in all of the above examples, though in differing degrees. In this sense, the most striking example of Cosmic Pessimism comes from outside of the metal genre altogether. It is by the Japanese multi-instrumentalist, poet, and mystic Keiji Haino. Haino's album *So, Black is Myself* takes the subtractive minimalism of Sunn O))) further, while borrowing techniques from everything from Butoh to Troubadour singing. Clocking in at just under 70 minutes, *So, Black is Myself* uses only a tone generator and voice. Its sole lyric is the title of the piece itself: *"Wisdom that will bless I, who live in the spiral joy born at the utter end of a black prayer."* The piece is brooding, rumbling, deeply sonorous, and meditative. Sometimes the tone generator and Haino's voice merge into one, while at other times they diverge. Haino's voice itself spans the tonal spectrum, from nearly subharmonic chant to an uncanny falsetto perhaps produced only by starving banshees. It is not only an example of the radically unhuman aspect of Cosmic Pessimism, the impersonal affect of dread described by Kierkegaard as "antipathic sympathy and sympathetic antipathy." *So, Black is Myself* also manages to be mystical at the same time that the individual performer is dissolved into a meshwork of tones – voice, body, and instrument variously existing in consonance and dissonance with each other.

QUÆSTIO II – On Whether There are Demons, and How to Know Them

ARTICULUS

That demons really exist seems to be verified by the cross-cultural acceptance of supernatural forces of some type, that may be rendered to varying degrees as animalistic or anthropomorphic, and that display a general antagonism towards all of humanity (and in some cases, the world itself). Scholarship in comparative mythology and religion has done much to reveal the similarities and the differences between demons of this type. The *jinn* in Islamic theology and pre-Islamic mythology, the *se'irim* of the Hebrew Bible, and the legion of evil spirits in the Judeo-Christian tradition, all testify to some type of supernatural antagonism that may manifest itself within theistic ways of understanding the world. Other claims have also been made for demon or demon-like equivalents in various African, Polynesian, and Native American folklore traditions, as well as in the Hindu and Buddhist pantheons (in the *Tibetan Book of the Dead*, for instance, one encounters, as part of the *Bardo* cycle, the "dawning of wrathful deities").

However, it seems that our technologically advanced, scientifically hegemonic, and religiously conservative post-millennium world leaves little room for something as fanciful as demons. At the most, such flights of the imagination are left to the culture industries, where demons swarm about (via advanced computer graphics) in films, television, and video games. Even within the culture industry, there is the subgenre of Satanic cinema – from "documentaries" such as *Häxan*, to Hollywood films like *The Exorcist*, to recent indie films like *House of the Devil*. In films like these, the elaborate scenes of exorcisms and possession serve to remind us that what we today classify as mental illness was, for an earlier era, a manifestation of the demonic.

Nevertheless, one must still account for the persistence of the figure of the demon, even as it is relegated to the fringes of genre fantasy, horror, and science fiction. One way of doing this is to understand the demon less in a strictly theological sense, in which the demon is the relation between the supernatural and natural, and to understand it in its cultural function as a way of thinking about the various relationships between human individuals and groups. In short, the figure of the demon, though it may not be accepted literally today, can be understood in an anthropological framework, as a metaphor for the nature of the human, and the relation of human to human (even when this relation is couched in terms of the boundary between human and non-human).

In fact, it would be possible to outline a cultural anthropology of the demon in Western culture with this perspective in mind. We could begin with the *daimōn* (δαίμων) in classical Greece, found in Hesiod and Homer as well as in the works of Plato. There the demon is not a malevolent or malefic figure, but an divine entity that may serve as a source of inspiration, but that may also serve to warn or to caution. When Socrates claims to always have by his side a "demon" (*daimonion*) that prevents him from taking the wrong course of action, he is invoking this more elemental meaning of the demon. The Greek demon is, in a sense, very much in keeping with the classical themes of human free will and destiny vis-à-vis the will of the gods.

The association of the demon with malevolent and malefic forces is most commonly made in early Christianity, though, as we've noted, there are arguments for its early development in early Judaic and Islamic theology as well. The archetypal example of this is the demon as tempter, as told in Athanasius' *Life of Antony*. While meditating in the desert, Anthony is repeatedly assaulted by demons, which take the form of everything from tempestuous winds to Satyrs and Centaurs. After closing himself off in a desert cave, Anthony is again assaulted by demons. "The demons, as if breaking through the building's four walls, and seeming to enter through them, were changed into the forms of beasts and reptiles."[2] Despite the pains he endures, Anthony's asceticism and prayer remains unfaltering, and the demonic assault is to no avail. This motif of immovable prayer against the temptations of the demon has also become something of an iconographic image of the demonic in Western art.

An interesting shift takes place once one moves into the clinical and medicalized view of Western modernity. In a 1923 article, "A Neurosis of Demonical Possession in the Seventeenth Century," Freud re-casts an account of possession in light of psychoanalysis' study of the workings of the unconscious. In terms of historical accounts of possession, the case study itself is unremarkable. It involves Christoph Haitzmann, a young

---

[2] Athanasius, *The Life of Antony*, trans. Robert C. Gregg (New York: HarperCollins, 1980), pp. 13-14.

painter who, in or around 1677, sees a priest, complaining of convulsions, hallucinations, and a sense of persecution. Aside from being an artist, the priest finds nothing wrong with Haitzmann – except, of course, that he may be in consort with a demon. Like the case study, Freud's analysis is also unremarkable. Tracing Haintzmann's delusions to the death of his father, Freud then remarks that the demon is a condensed "father-substitute" – at once a replacement for Haitzmann's mourned loss, as well as a crisis brought about by the absence of the father as a figure of authority. As per the standard psychoanalytic reading, the demon is taken to be an externalized projection, and the so-called possession really a form of therapeutic purging for Haitzmann himself.

We might even attempt a further permutation, in which the demon is neither purely theological or psychological, but sociological. Here the political aspects of the demon, as the stand-in for a threatening Other, come to the fore. The demon becomes a name, a place-holder, a designation that signifies at once that which is outside and, because of this, that which is a threat. Exemplary in this regard is recent scholarship in comparative religious studies. Elaine Pagel's widely-read *The Origin of Satan* makes the clearest point: the demon is inseparable from a process of demonization, and this process is as much political as it is religious. Whether, as in Pagel's study, the demonic refers to pagans (the threat from outside), or to non-Christian Jews (the boundary between outside and inside), or, finally, to acts of heresy within Christianity (the threat from inside), all follow this motif of naming an Other.

If the demon is taken in this anthropological sense as the relation of the human to the non-human (however this non-human is understood), then we can see how the demon historically passes through various phases: there is the classical demon, which is elemental, and at once a help and sometimes a hindrance (*"the demon beside me . . ."*); there is the Medieval demon, a supernatural and intermediary being that is a tempter (*"demons surround me . . . "*); a modern demon, rendered both natural and scientific through psychoanalysis, and internalized within the machinations of the unconscious (*"I am a demon to myself..."*); and finally a contemporary demon, in which the social and political aspects of antagonism are variously attributed to the Other in relationships of enmity (*"demons are other people"*).

SED CONTRA

Let us return to the traditional, Christian-theological premise of the demon – demons are, generally speaking, both malevolent and malefic. They are understood as supernatural beings that intend to do evil to humanity, and do so through supernatural means. Whether they be rendered as a monstrous, chimeric creatures, or as invisible and immaterial dark forces, the demon often inhabits the edges of the human understanding of the world. This twofold characteristic – an antagonism towards the human, and some form of supernatural mediation – are a key part of the theological concept of the demon. By the time one arrives at modern psychoanalysis, the antagonism is internalized (perhaps via some personal trauma) and the mediation is medicalized (for example, as a form of clinical paranoia). Even in such cases, however, the manifestation of the phenomena in question are taken as if the antagonism is external, and as if the mediation comes from the outside. This twofold character remains, if only in a more secular and more scientific framework. The "as if" is important, since for a previous era the "as if" was taken quite simply "as is."

In the interpretations of the demon above, the demon functions as a metaphor for the human – both in the sense of the human's ability to comprehend itself, as well as the relations between one human being and another. The demon is not really a supernatural creature, but an anthropological motif through which we human beings project, externalize, and represent the darker side of the human to ourselves. While this may serve a certain therapeutic function, something is lost in this anthropological interpretation of the demon, and that is the way in which the antagonism to central to the demon is also an non-human antagonism, an antagonism that is beyond human comprehension – not natural but supernatural, not merely physical but metaphysical. But how is the traditional Christian-theological demon non-human, when again and again in both sacred texts as well as treatises of demonology, demons are represented in decidedly anthropomorphic ways?

One way of understanding the non-human aspect of the demon is to understand the demon less in a strictly theological sense, in which the demon is an intermediary creature between the supernatural and natural, and to understand it in its ontological function as a way of thinking about the relation of the human to that which is non-human. This vague, latter term – the non-human – can, of course, have a wide range of meanings, from the rock or the chair to the black depths of the cosmos itself. And we as human beings certainly have a panoply of ways of relating to the non-human, be it via science, technology, politics, or religion. But the non-human remains, by definition, a limit; it designates both that which we stand in relation to and that which remains forever inaccessible to us. This limit is the unknown, and the unknown, as genre horror reminds us, is often a source of fear or dread.

Thus, in contrast to the anthropological interpretation of the demon, we can consider another one that is *mythological*. By this term we imply more than the human understanding of the human, and instead move outwards to the human understanding of the world. The mythological interpretation of the demon takes place less by the use of metaphor, and more by the use of allegory, in which the very story of our ability or inability to comprehend the world and cosmos is encapsulated in the ritual acts of invasion, possession, metamorphosis, and exorcism.

This comes through more clearly in one of the classic Biblical accounts of demonic possession, that of the so-called Gerasene demon. Slightly different accounts are given in *Mark* 5 and *Luke* 8, but the basics of the parable are the same: Jesus, with his followers, travels from Galilee to the Gerasene region (in northern current-day Jordan). There Jesus is met by the local villagers, who appeal to him to heal an old man possessed by demons. The possessed man, it is said, roams about the tombs without clothing or shelter. When he is shackled by the villagers, he enters into a frenzy and breaks free. At night he screams aloud and cuts himself with stones. Jesus confronts the possessed man, who likewise appeals to Jesus to cure him. As part of the exorcism, Jesus commands the name of the demon possessing the old man: "Then Jesus asked him, 'What is your name?' 'My name is Legion,' he replied, 'for we are many.'"[3] The name "Legion" (λεγων) is tricky, for it is not clear from the passage whether it is a single demon speaking in many voices, or if it is a multitude of demons speaking in a single voice. Indeed, the very name "Legion" appears to devolve upon itself,

---

[3] *Mark* 5:9-10, New International Version. Stephanus New Testament version consulted for Koine Greek text.

the name of the Many naming itself as One. Jesus then casts the demons out of the body of the old man, and into a herd of swine in a nearby hill. The herd of swine, now possessed, are driven into a state of frenzy and rush over the side of a cliff into the sea below to their death. After this rather dramatic episode, something interesting happens: the villagers, witnessing the entire spectacle, become fearful of Jesus and his healing powers. With some urgency they politely ask Jesus and his followers to leave the village, which they do.

In this parable the demons manifest themselves in three ways, each an example of the limits of the human to comprehend the non-human. First, within the possessed man are a multitude of demons. Demonic possession itself transgresses the normal relationship between the One and the Many (one person = one body). It is also an affront to and parody of the Trinity, in which a single One is incarnated in Three. God as Creator creates many creatures. As creatures they are at once linked to God through the act of creation. Yet, as creatures, they are also separated from God in their being mortal and rooted in the changes associated with temporality. The multitude of demons in the parable above occupy the individual human creature – that highest of creatures – and turn him into a mere animal-like thing. The iconography of the passage is striking – the true nature of the demons, we presume, is revealed by the choice of their receptacle in a herd of lowly beasts. But throughout the parable, the only real indication we have of this multitude of demons is this enigmatic resounding of the word "Legion." In a philosophical sense, that the demons choose to present themselves via voice and sound – at once present and absent – is noteworthy.

These two manifestations of the demon – the demons in the old man and the herd of animals – lead to a third type, which is the word-of-mouth among the people, which itself spreads like a disease. Jesus' demonstration of his divine sovereign and medical powers instills a certain horror in the people, resulting in his effectively being deported. We might take a decidedly modern view of this scene and suggest that the threat posed by the demons is not simply a topological one having to do with the proper relation between the One and the Many, and neither is it to do with the proper relation between Creator and creature. There is another element here, which is the way in which the demonic also challenges divine sovereignty. The demonic challenges the divine in its refusal to be organized at all. We do not know how many demons there are, nor even if it is more than one voice that speaks "Legion." We only know that it is more than one, and that it may be something other than "Many," the latter term still denoting a potentially countable entity. The demons are, in a sense, more than Many, but never One.

Examples of demonic activity occur throughout the New Testament, though in it demons are by no means represented in the same way. For example, the famous scene of the apocalypse in *Revelations* not only features a battle between angels and demons, but it also portrays avenging angels that tend to look a lot like demons. These supernatural creatures are anthropomorphized, and they even have their own technology: trumpets, tempests, and "bowls of plague" come forth in the apocalyptic upsurge. In these scenes the demons/angels have as their sole function a religious-juridical relation to the human (either to damn or to save them). The various symbolic devices, from scales and seals to bowls, are the technologies for the end of the world. Here the demons are a form of *mediated presence*.

By contrast, the exorcism scene from the Gospels portrays a demon that is unmediated and yet only embodied – the demons called "Legion" are never present in themselves, but only via some form of earthly embodiment (the old man, the herd of pigs, the wind, the sea). In a sense, they are strangely pantheistic, announcing themselves only indirectly. Hence their embodiment is also a disembodiment, in the sense that they are wandering spirits – their movement happens more by demonic contagion than by divine inspiration. Demons are here a form of *immediate absence.*

While the anthropological meaning of the demon remains ensconced within its human-centric, therapeutic solipsism (e.g. "why do we do the things we do?"), the mythological meaning focuses on the limits of the human ability to know that which is non-human. At its limit is the idea of the absolutely "dark" demon – the demon that remains absolute unknowable to use as human beings, but which nevertheless seems to act upon us, perhaps through a malevolence we can only call "bad luck" or "misfortune."

RESPONSIO

If the anthropological demon is an attempt to reveal the nature of the human to the human, then we can say that the mythological demon is an attempt to reveal the non-human to the human. Both, however, come across certain limitations, precisely because of the human point-of-view. The human is always relating either to itself or to the world. And these two types of relations overlap with each other: the human can only understand the human by transforming it into an object to relate to (psychology, sociology), while the human can only relate to the objective world itself by transforming the world into something familiar, accessible, or intuitable in human terms (biology, geology, cosmology).

This leaves one unexplored avenue open, which is the perspective of the non-human itself. As thinking, embodied beings unable to fully detach ourselves from the subject-object relations that constitute us, this is undoubtedly a paradoxical move. In fact, it is doomed from the start. Nevertheless it deserves to be stated, even if beyond it there can only be silence, nothingness, or emptiness. In the parable of the Gerasene demons, the demons named "Legion" were, in themselves, defined by several properties: they were neither One nor Many but somewhere in between; they were fully immanent with the world and creatures of the world (almost pantheistically so); and, most importantly, they in themselves were never present, never a discrete thing that one could point to – the demons named "Legion" were really, in themselves, "nothing."

Perhaps there is a meaning of the demonic that has little to do with the human at all – *and this indifference is what constitutes its demonic character*. If the anthropological demon (the human relating to itself) functioned via metaphor, and if the mythological demon (the human relating or not relating to the non-human) functioned via allegory, then perhaps there is a third demon, which is more ontological, or really "meontological" (having to do with non-being rather than being). Given that, for us as human beings, there is no simple "going over" to the side of the non-human, it would seem that the mode best suited to this third type of demon is something like metonymy. The demon is, then, a way of talking about the perspective of the non-human, with all the contradictions this implies. For the meontological demon, affirmation is negation, and thinking about its being is the same as thinking about nothingness.

This is brought forward with great subtlety in Dante's *Inferno*, one of the classic depictions of the demonic. However, there is not simply one type of demon in the *Inferno*, and the central drama of the *Inferno* is not good vs. evil, but in the tensions within the *Inferno* itself. For instance, one can identify at least three types of demons in the *Inferno*. First there is, at the center and lowest point of the underworld, the figure of Lucifer, the arch-demon. This takes place in the final scene of the *Inferno*, where Dante the pilgrim is led by his guide Virgil to the center of the underworld. Dante (the poet) uses the word Dis in the poem, an alternate name for Pluto, the god of the classical underworld, to refer to the giant, grotesque, brooding arch-emperor ("emperor of all these realms of gloom").[4]

From Gustave Doré's engravings for the *Commedia* of Dante (1861-1868).

---

[4] Dante Alighieri, *Inferno*, trans. Robin Kirkpatrick (New York: Penguin, 2006), XXXIV: 28. As Charles Singleton notes in the Princeton commentary, this is also the name used by Virgil in the *Aeneid*.

Here we have the counter-sovereign, who is, like the divine sovereign, is centralized and transcendent with respect to that which he governs. However, this counter-sovereign demon actually does very little in the long journey that constitutes the *Inferno*. The scene is depicted with great detail by the 19th century artist Gustave Doré. Immobilized in the frozen waters of the underworld, this counter-sovereign demon is condemned to repeat the same cycle of transgression and blasphemy against the Creator.

Distinct from this, there are the multitude of demons found peppered throughout the different circles of the underworld. An example are the so-called Malebranche demons found in the 8th Circle. These are "demons" in the more modern, Faustian sense – they are torturers, tricksters, and tempters.

From Gustave Doré's engraving for the *Commedia* of Dante (1861-1868).

The Malebrance demons are less the giant, majestic counter-sovereign, and more a roving pack, a demonic gang. They operate according to the basic rules of the underworld, and are more decentralized, their power emanating from the rule of the counter-sovereign.

Contrasted to these two types of demons – the counter-sovereign Dis, and the Malebrance demons – there is a third, which comes near the beginning of the *Inferno*. This is the Second Circle, the Circle of the Lustful. In a dramatic passage, Dante-the-pilgrim is lead by his guide Virgil to a precipice where, for the first time in the narrative, he encounters the strange and dark atmosphere of the demonic:

> I came to a place where no light shone at all,
> bellowing like the sea racked by a tempest,
> when warring winds attack it from both sides.
>
> The infernal storm (*bufera infernal*), eternal in its rage,
> sweeps and drives the spirits with its blast:
> it whirls them, lashing them with punishment.
>
> When they are swept back past their place of judgment,
> then come the shrieks, laments, and anguished cries;
> there they blaspheme God's almighty power.

To this place the lustful have been sent, all "those who make reason slave to appetite." The mass of bodies, blown back and forth by the wind, prompt a comparison to the swarms of bird flocks:

> and as the wings of starlings in the winter
> bear them along in wide-spread, crowded flocks,
> so does that wind propel the evil spirits (*spiriti mali*);
>
> now here, then there, and up and down, it drives them

with never any hope to comfort them –
hope not of rest but even of suffering less.

We soon learn that this tempestuous scene is not the backdrop for some new genre of demons, but that the wind, the rain, and the storm itself is the demon. This "black wind" (*aura nera*) is at once invisible and yet dramatically manifest, coursing through the swarming bodies of the damned.

One of the images from Doré's illustrations depicts the well-known scene in which two of the spirits – Paolo and Francesca – emerge from the swarm of bodies to tell their tale of tragic love. Dante-the-pilgrim, moved by the scene and their story, is overcome and faints, next to Virgil who is by his side. But what is equally interesting in the image is the way that Doré makes the bodies of Paolo and Francesca barely stand out from the amorphous background of swarming spirits, which seems to recede back into infinity. Indeed, in certain areas the bodies appear to merge into the backdrop of the storm itself.

From Gustave Doré's engraving for the *Commedia* of Dante (1861-1868).

HIDEOUS GNOSIS

In this scene there is neither a fixed and majestic counter-sovereign, nor a roving gang of Faustian demons. There is only the strange, immanent, and fully distributed "life-force" of this black wind. The spirits of the Lustful in this circle also dissolve into the elemental swarming of the storm and the wind. It is paradoxically the most manifest form of life (indeed, Dante faints before its force), and yet it is also the most empty (the demonic storm is not a discrete thing, much less a discrete body, it is everywhere but nowhere). Arguably, this last scene puts forth the most difficult view of the demon – not a transcendent, governing cause, and not an emanating, radiating flow – but a concept of the demonic that is fully immanent, and yet never fully present. This kind of demon is at once pure force and flow, but, not being a discrete thing in itself, it is also pure nothingness.

Generally speaking, the *Inferno* is of interest not simply due to the panoply of monsters that inhabit its pages, but because of the way in which it carefully stratifies different types of demonic being and non-being. Within the paths, rivers, caverns, and fortresses of the *Inferno* all boundaries collapse: there are human bodies melting into dead trees, rivers flowing with blood, and entire cities populated with the living dead. The motif of possession in the *Inferno* demonstrates this: demonic possession is not just the possession of living beings, but includes the possession of the non-living as well. Demons possess not only human beings and animals, but the very landscape, the very terrain of the underworld. Demonic possession in the *Inferno* is not just teratological, but also geological and even climatological.

QUÆSTIO III – On Demonology, and Whether it is a Respectable Field of Study

ARTICULUS

Demonology is commonly understood to no longer be of contemporary relevance; it is an unfortunate and anachronistic offshoot of late Medieval and early Renaissance theology, the stuff of the imaginative fancy of modern horror films. The term "demonology" itself is most often understood in a historical sense, as the study and classification of demons (often inclusive of activities such as witchcraft and necromancy), and which was directly tied to the long, dark history of the witch-hunts and persecutions of heretics in Europe between the 15th-17th centuries. While Christian theologians from Augustine to Aquinas had written extensively about the nature of evil prior to this period, the idea that a distinct field of study devoted to the topic – as well as to its practical application in combating and rooting out evil – does not really emerge until the late 15th century. An often-cited reference point is the papal bull *Summis desiderantes affectibus* (1484), issued by Pope Innocent VII in response to growing concerns that heretical activities, including witchcraft, constitute a serious threat to the unification of Church authority across the continent. The bull is noteworthy for several reasons, the foremost being that it confirmed the existence of witches, witchcraft, and the activities of all those who "have abandoned themselves to demons," through rituals undertaken "at the instigation of the Enemy of Mankind." If identifying an enemy as an enemy is to give that enemy strength, then this identification of witchcraft and demonic dealings would proved to be a double-edged sword. Of the countless trials and executions that took place under the banner of the Inquisition (modern estimates by historians range from

40,000 to 100,000 executions in continental Europe alone, between 1500-1700), the scope of the witch-trials broadened, in some cases to including the mere defense against an accusation of witchcraft as itself constituting an act of heresy.

The bull *Summis desiderantes affectibus* not only identified a threat, it also made recommendations for dealing with that threat. It gave Church inquisitors such as Heinrich Kramer and Jacob Sprenger the authority to legally seek out, put to trial, and execute those suspected of dealing with demons and practicing witchcraft. Roughly two years after the publication of the bull, Kramer and Sprenger publish the book that has become the hallmark of the witch-hunt manual: the *Malleus Maleficarum* (1486; tr. "Hammer of Witches"). Much of the *Malleus Maleficarum* is typical of the writing on witchcraft and demonology of the period. There are references to the writings of the Church Fathers and Scholastic theologians on the dangers of evil and evil-doing demons. There are also attempts to distinguish and classify the different kinds of demonic activity. And there are a number of case studies of witchcraft, demonic possession, and other acts of *malefica* that serve to paint a picture of the real threat at hand.

What makes the *Malleus Maleficarum* unique, however, is its practical orientation. It is not a work of theological speculation, as is Aquinas' *De malo* (ca. 1270; tr. "On Evil"). Neither is it an attempt at systematic classification, as is Francesco-Maria Guazzo's *Compendium Maleficarum* (1608; tr. "Encyclopedia of Witchcraft"). It is, quite literally, a instruction manual, clearly demonstrated by the book's three parts: Part I, which argues that witches and witchcraft really exist, and are a threat; Part II, which deals with how witches and witchcraft can be detected and exposed; and Part III, which outlines the protocols for carrying out a trial, sentencing, and punishment or execution.

Title pages from a 1580 edition of the *Malleus Maleficarum* and from a 1626 edition of the *Compendium Maleficarum*.

Of particular interest is the role played by 16th century medicine in demonology manuals like the *Malleus Maleficarum*. One role medicine played was in the cultivation of a general miasmatic or contagion-theory of demonic possession. In this pre-modern understanding of contagion, the demon is conceptualized in much the same way we saw earlier – as a paradoxical manifestation that is, in itself, "nothing" or non-being. This is illustrated in the *Malleus Maleficarum* in the three main types of demonic possession, each exhibiting anomalous symptoms that – in the argument of the demonologist – can be causally traced to some sort of commerce with a demon. At the first level is there is psycho-physiological possession, in which the demonic spirit invades and affects the body itself (with symptoms ranging from temporary disability and incapacitation, to impotence, infertility, and eroto-mania, to epilepsy, narcolepsy, and melancholia). At a second level there are cases of epidemiological possession, which affects the relation between body and environment (plague, leprosy, mass hysteria, even mob behavior). Finally, at a third level one finds a more abstract, climatological possession, in which demons possess not only the living and animate, but the non-living and inanimate as well (unnatural or anomalous changes in weather, affected livestock or crops, sudden famine or flood).

Added to this epistemological role of medicine is another role, which is juridical. Though the *Malleus Maleficarum* is a decidedly single-minded text, aiming without hesitation at the extermination of all witchcraft activity, it does make minimal allowances for natural, as opposed to supernatural, causes of witchcraft (which are in no way less punishable). While there was rarely any question as to the supernatural character of the witch or witchcraft activity in question, the exact cause of the said activity could be open to interpretation. There may be, for example, a supernatural cause producing a natural symptom. Such symptoms could be classified as either illusion or illness. If illusion, then the question was whether the accused is intentionally using some sort of trickery, and for what reason (e.g. for gain of money, revenge, jealousy, etc.). If illness, then the question was what type of illness, the vaguely-defined illness of epilepsy, hysteria, and melancholy being the most commonly-cited explanations. The role of medicine here is less to develop knowledge about demonic possession, and more to arbitrate – within the juridical context of the trial – the boundary between the natural and supernatural. Interestingly, it is this role that would be reinforced by later writers more skeptical of the witch-hunts and the mass paranoia they produced. Note, however, that a natural explanation of a phenomenon such as necromancy or possession in no way rules out the presence of the supernatural – in many instances it simply serves as yet another route towards the inevitable sentence.

Although witch-hunting manuals proliferated throughout the period, the *Malleus Maleficarum* set a new standard, encompassing theology (Part I), medicine (Part II), and law (Part III) into a single work. The result was not only a new set of juridical procedures, but an new discourse and way of thinking about the demon in terms of the non-human. This is also evident in the early Renaissance debates over the status of demons and demonic possession, in treatises such as Johann Weyer's *De praestigiis daemonium* (1563; tr. "On the Trickery of Demons"), Jean Bodin's *Démonomanie des sorciers* (1580; tr. ("The Demonmania of Witches"), and Reginald Scot's *Discoverie of Witchcraft* (1584).

Weyer's *De praestigiis daemonium* is noteworthy as being one of the few treatises that expresses criticism of the excesses of the with-hunts and witchcraft trials. While Weyer did admit the real existence of witches, witchcraft, and demons, he also allowed for cases in which individuals were helplessly deluded by demons (thinking that their hallucinations were real), as well as cases of simple trickery. As Weyer ominously notes, real demons do not need us to carry out their acts of ill-will – in fact, it is the height of vanity to suppose that we as human beings are in any way necessary for them. Be that as it may, it is noteworthy that Weyer, who studied under the scientist and reputed magician Cornelius Agrippa, spent most of his life as a physician, and this impacts his allowance for medical-psychological explanations of witchcraft. He notes, with biting sarcasm, that "such rare and severe symptoms often arise in diseases that stem from natural causes but are immediately attributed to witchcraft by men of no scientific experience and little faith."[5] The *De praestigiis daemonium* also contains a number of indictments against the excessive use of torture and maltreatment of accused witches – at least before a proper examination of a case can be carried out.

Bodin's *Démonomanie* is a direct counter-attack to Weyer. Bodin, a Carmelite monk, member of Parliament, and professor of law, is mostly known in political philosophy for his massive work *Les Six Livres de la République*, a work which contains an early theorization of absolute state sovereignty. Written in order to aid judges in witchcraft cases, Bodin's *Démonomanie* is a disturbing work that advocates, among other things, the legal use of torture to elicit confessions of guilt, including the use of techniques such as cautery. It also contains one of the early legal definitions of a witch, as one "who, knowing God's law, tries to bring about some act through an agreement with the Devil." It also contains a veritable litany of the anti-human antagonism of demons: "...all demons are malevolent, deceiving, posturing enemies of humanity..."[6] The *Démonomanie* never wavers in its assertion of the religious and political threat of witchcraft – that is, the threat that witchcraft posed to statecraft. The conviction in the *Démonomanie* appears to derive in part from Bodin's own experience as a judge, in which he saw a number of witchcraft trials (and purportedly showed no

---

[5] *On Witchcraft: An Abridged Translation of Johann Weyer's De praestigiis daemonium* (trans. John Shea, ed. Benjamin Kohl and H.C. Erik Midelfort, Pegasus Press), Bk. V, ch. 28, p. 238.

[6] *De la démonomanie des sorciers* (Paris: Jacques du Puys, 1580), Bk. II, ch. 8, p. 237. The passage reads "...tous les Demons sont malings, menteurs, imposteurs, ennemis du genre humain." However Bodin continues with the complicated caveat "...et qu'ils n'ont plus de puissance que Dieu leur en permet."

hesitation in torturing children and invalids to gain a confession).

If Weyer represents the attitude of temperance towards witchcraft (under the guise of medicine), and if Bodin represents the conservative retrenchment (under the guise of law), then Scot's *Discoverie of Witchcraft* takes the next step, which is to question the validity of the entire affair altogether. To the role of medicine in Weyer, and the role of law in Bodin, we have the role of skepticism in Scot. While Weyer and Bodin are on opposite sides of the fence politically, theologically they both remain committed to the existence of supernatural forces and the conflict paradigm of good vs. evil. Scot, who had the advantage of relative financial independence, was neither beholden to the Church nor to science in his opinions – though the *Discoverie of Witchcraft* was printed at his own expense, was unregistered, and did not contain the publisher's name. Most likely spurred on by a series of controversial witch trails in England in the early 1580s, Scot's treatise is much more sarcastic, even humorous, in its criticisms. He attacks both the pretenses of witches and witchcraft, dismissing them as trickery (either on others or on oneself), as well as the "extreme and intolerable tyranny" of the inquisitors and judges. In a sense, Scot's treatise is a sort of clearing-house for the very concepts of the demon, and indeed of the supernatural itself. As if to accuse both witches and inquisitors of a too-provincial, all-too-human mindset, the *Discoverie of Witchcraft* suggests that, in so far as there is a concept of the demon, it has to be one of which we can have little or no knowledge.

SED CONTRA

The debates surrounding witchcraft and demonology are instructive in that they often revolve around our ability to adequately comprehend the supernatural – be it divine or demonic. In particular, the question of the demon tends to oscillate, from highly anthropomorphic Satyrs to the more abstract and obscure demons that contagiously pass in the breath from person to person. Much of the confusion of the early demonology treatises centers on how to verify the existence of a demon, when, by definition, they are rarely self-evident to the human observer. In cases where demonic possession cannot be distinguished from medical illness, on which side should one stand? To the 21st century mind, the question is absurd. But for an era in which the lines between magic, science, and witchcraft were blurry, such questions were not only religious and political, but philosophical too. To the culture of the early Renaissance, the demon presents a limit to the empiricism of the unknown, something that can only be verified through contradictions – an absent manifestation, an unnatural creature, a demonic malady.

Such contradictions stretch the limits of language. Indeed, one of the by-products of the flurry of writings on demonology was the development of a new language and a new set of concepts for thinking about the supernatural. Certainly this language and these concepts were informed by theology, but, in describing the effects of possession, in evoking the scene of the witches' sabbath, and in imagining a world swarming with malefic entities, a certain *poetics* of the demon was also needed. Demonology – whether it aims to convince or to criticize – is as much a rhetorical activity as it is a theological or juridical one. Thus, in contrast to the view of demonology as theological, we can briefly consider a poetics of the demon as equally central to the concept of the demon.

If one were to outline a poetics of the demon, one could begin by thinking about the motif of the demonic and its literary representation. More specifically, one could understand the demon as represented via different motifs. For example the narrative technique of the journey – so common in the history of world literature – is a key feature of Dante's *Commedia*, as Dante the pilgrim journeys from the dark circles of Hell, through the conical spiral of Purgatory, to the celestial geometries of Paradise, along the way undergoing various trials of his own. This is a topological motif, in which we encounter various people, places, and creatures. The demonic is here symbolically inscribed by a particular locale (for instance, the way that the different circles of Hell contain different classes of demonic punishments for different sins).

The same follows for other narrative motifs. There is the battle, such as one finds in Milton's *Paradise Lost*, and, following upon (and critiquing) Milton, as one finds in scenes from William Blake's prophecies. Here we find the structure of agonism, with the demonic ensnared in an eternal struggle or conflict. Then there is the motif of the pact, the black bargain with a demon that at once liberates and imprisons the human character who signs their name in blood. This is a juridical and economic structure, most commonly associated with the Faust story and its literary incarnations by such authors as Marlowe and Goethe – I give you my soul, and in exchange, you give me…everything. The pact often overlaps with another narrative motif, which is that of the ritual. The infamous depictions of the Black Mass in novels such as Huysmans' *Là-bas* or Dennis Wheatley's *The Devil Rides Out* involve a whole series of sacrilegious acts that, at the same time, express a certain sanctity of evil. The demonic is the counter-divine, at once negating the divine while sanctifying the demonic. Wheatley's "black" novels are particularly noteworthy, for the protagonist De Richleau often uses both ancient and modern-scientific knowledge in his battle against demons and dark forces, continuing the "psychic detective" genre inaugurated by authors such as Sheridan Le Fanu. Finally, there is the more modern, technological motif of the magical artifact, the dark invention that signals a new kind of apocalypse. Science fiction works such as Fritz Leiber's *Gather, Darkness!* and James Blish's *Faust Aleph-Null*, written in the shadow of world war and mass extinction, suggest a ominous affinity between technology and the supernatural. In Leiber's novel a futuristic Papacy utilizes a whole panoply of special-effects technologies to both ensure the fidelity of the masses to the hegemony of the Church. Against them a demonic underworld of witches, warlocks, and familiars carry out their revolutionary cause. By contrast, Blish's novel suggests that with weapons of mass destruction, a renewed Faustian pact has been made, with quantum physics as a form of necromancy. In these 20th century works, the demonic plays different roles, either as a revolutionary counter-power, or as an essentially unknowable force beyond human comprehension and human control.

One of the striking commonalities between works of this type is that nearly all of them seem to follow an unwritten rule – the demonic antagonist must always "lose" in the end. Certainly this would seem to follow the moral economy of the literary form of the novel or the epic poem (similar to the requisite happy ending of a studio film). But one always feels a little let down by this *deus ex machina*. Goethe's Faust goes all the way in his demonic explorations, only to later repent and – in Part II – saved by virtue of divine grace. Similarly there is Blake's famous statement about Milton's *Paradise Lost* – that the latter was of the Devil's party without knowing it. Here one finds the problem of "being-on-the-side-of" the demonic, when the demonic is really unknown and, perhaps, unknowable. However, the failure of the demonic antagonists in literary examples like these is perhaps less a testament to the victorious nature of good, and more an indication of a certain moral economy of the unknown. By the end of Goethe's *Faust* we know no more or less of the demonic than when we started, in spite of having the wool pulled over our eyes.

RESPONSIO

Here again we arrive at the concept of the demon as a limit-concept, a limit for thought that is constituted not by being or becoming, but by non-being, or nothingness. And here we should state what we have been hinting at all along, which is that in contrast to the theology of the demon, or the poetics of the demon, there is something more basic still that has to do with the ideas of negation and nothingness – hence we should really think of the demon as an ontological problem (not theology, not poetry, but philosophy).

True, demonology is a theological phenomenon, tied up with historical debates about the nature of demons, and the politics surrounding the with-hunts. True, demonology is also a cultural phenomenon, as the ongoing poetic, literary, cinematic, and video game examples demonstrate. But demonology ceases to be interesting if it is taken as being "merely" historical, or "only" a fiction. If demonology is to be thought in a philosophical register, then it would have to function as a kind of philosopheme that brings together a cluster of ideas that have, for some time, served as problematic areas for philosophy itself: negation, nothingness, and the non-human.

What would such an approach to demonology look like? To begin with, demonology would have to be distinguished from anthropology (the demon as stand-in for the human) and from pure ontology (the demon as stand-in for the pair being/non-being). Denying the anthropological view means considering the world as not simply the world-for-us (the limit of the human). Likewise denying the ontological view means considering the unreliability of the principle of sufficient reason (the insufficiency of being). A philosophical demonology would therefore have to be "against" the human being – both the "human" part as well as the "being" part.

Perhaps we can come up with a new term for this way of thinking – *demontology*. If anthropology is predicated on a division between the personal and the impersonal ("man" and cosmos), then a demontology would collapse them (impersonal affects, cosmic suffering). If ontology deals with the minimal relation being/non-being, then demontology would have to undertake the thought of nothingness (a negative definition), but a nothingness that is also not simply non-being (a privative definition). Finally, a demontology would have to distinguish itself from the moral, juridical, and cosmic framework of Christian demonology (moral law, temptation, transgression, sin, punishment, salvation, etc.). And here demontology comes up against one of the greatest challenges for thought today, and it is, in many ways, a Nietzschean one – how does one rethink "politics" in the absence of the human, and without being?

Again, we run up against all sorts of obstacles, in part because a philosophical demonology does not exist – or not yet. Should one then create a lineage, citing predecessors of this type of Cosmic Pessimism? But here an interminable game of inclusion and exclusion begins. Should one include classical philosophers, such as Heraclitus? Should one include works in the tradition of "darkness mysticism" or negative theology? And then what of the great works of spiritual and philosophical crisis, from Kierkegaard to Cioran or Weil? We've already mentioned Schopenhauer, but then are we obliged to also consider

Nietzsche, Bataille, Blanchot, or Shestov? Then again, would there not be a basic problem in positing or hoping for the existence of a field dedicated to negation and nothingness? Is it possible for one to make the claim that demontology exists, without becoming ensnared in an endless theater of the absurd? Perhaps the only thing for certain is if something like a demontology could exist, it would not be made any more respectable because of its existence – for nothing is more frowned upon than nothing.

BLACK CONFESSIONS AND ABSU-LUTION
Niall Scott, Sin Eater

Black Confessions and absolution. This is why we are here and this is why we are absent. We are concerned with the value and function of confessions; the Celtic confessor tradition through to medieval confession, its value and the lament of absence in contemporary society. Now manifest in Black metal, Black Metal Theory brings back a confessory space, a black confessory space, but in its void leads to a rather different absolution, an Absu-lution.

The Didache, 4, verse 14 written around AD 70 urged: "Confess your sins in church and do not go up to your prayer with an evil conscience. This is the way of life On the Lord's day gather together, break bread and give thanks, after confessing your transgressions so that your sacrifice may be pure."

A counter confession in a paragraph by Nergal Behemoth, Evangellion 2009 AD: "Tyranny preys on fear. Most human beings are slaves of abhorrence, anxiety cowardice and despair. The communion they partake in is abomination and the names of these sacraments is a stupor which ends in final sleep of the soul. The bounds are so painful and the chains are so strong that they prefer to humbly kneel before the reality with eyes fixed on the cold floor of the churches, town halls, and banks. If any of them think we are here to rebel for the sake of rebellion they are mistaken. Our goal is to bring fire from heaven and hell in order to purify the corrupted state of being .We fear nothing. Our aim is to rise and awake, to transform fear into philosophical awe of the universe which heavily falls on our fragile bodies and crushes or souls with the totality of experience."

Absu tell us that:

> "Those Of The Void Will Re-Enter"
> Thousand after thousand
> The years of tradition linger
> For the wisdom of magic(k)
> The supra catalyst swells
> Servants of the arcane order
> The hypnotized beings
> Can you commemorate?
> The burden of ignorance
>
> Clad in robes imprinted with spells
> Regress time – degenerate
> Founders of mankind,
> Come lay your claim
> Revert – Annunaki
> Those of the void will re-enter
> Clad in robes imprinted with spells
> Regress time – degenerate
> Founders of mankind . . .
> Regress time - Regress time
> Those of the void have re-entered!

Thus the words of Absu.

Confession, from the Greek *homologein*: is a public liturgical event. It means to speak at the same time, or to say the same thing. It is to repeat words to repeat words: *glossan homologein*.

Even further than this, it concerns having the members of a group of people say the same thing. It is further both an acknowledgement and also a profession, a concurrence of wills, and very much a communitarian phrase involving an event. It is also an agreement amongst others. These statements cannot be reverted and in Greek history had a binding component in Athenian law.

In the Christian tradition confession involves two elements: the confession of faith and the confession of sin. Of faith it is a public declaration of belief and its binding nature in an eschatological sense. It relates to the *homologein* as an expression of declaration in unison, as binding as it was in the Athenian law. Earlier based on the Jewish tradition of the process leading to Yom Kippur holds the confession of guilt and fasting, paired with abstinence: a void of prohibitions. The sins of the people on the day of atonement were absolved by laying hands on a live goat which carries away the sins of the people; Christ then becomes the eternal substitution of the goat.

But in Baphomet and black metal the goat, rather than being crucified still dwells among us. The black metal event, the scene, the movement, persists in dealing with the misery of the human condition where Christianity gave it over to be privatised, individualised and removed from the public sphere into the confession box where one is neither alive not dead, but suspended surrendering control. This is surrendered to give way; to gain either priestly control over the people or to hide misery in the secrets sphere of the soul. This is as much a control over the power of language as the power over souls. As Michel Foucault tells us in The History of Sexuality, that which is confessed- confession of that which has become secret and forbidden moves from the act of confession to becoming discourse. Desire is transformed into discourse, but the language used neutralises the content of which the confession refers to. Derrida agrees with this point regarding language neutralising the event. Does this not contradict the power of language as the original creative force? Instead of speaking things into being, speaking together removes things from being, at least from being effective. Such is the effect of neutralising. Where language points to the event to the sin and represents the sin so effectively, then Certain Language is then forbidden. It is removed from the public sphere to the confession box; to the therapeutic couch, to the private stereo headphone; behind closed doors it moves into the private sphere more and more.

The reaction to this is to indulge in uncontrolled scandal to "tell everything", to make that which is secret public. To spew and to vomit, to vent in voluminous cacophonies into the vacuum created by this corrupting act of the privatisation of confession. So the form of the original confession in the Christian tradition was communal, public and binding, until the Jesuit empty box introduced a veil of censorship, a canopy of the unseen over the lips and eyelids of the living dead, where they repeat their words over and over again: *glossan homologein*.

Instead of the power of prohibition and censorship Black Metal Theory serves to increase and expand more and more on that which has been forbidden. Thus we can locate and understand the same thing of the venting of anti-Christian or even antireligious sentiments in Black Metal's early years and this continuing theme, but in its time this will come to an end. Marduk's Morgan In the subterranean voice of the Metal Hammer is on this path: "We've crushed Christianity for so many albums and the way that we've done it has ensured that there is no power for Christianity over us any more. Black metal is about a feeling and a devotion . . . I believe in the power of performing music in front of people. I believe in being there. Performing is a magical ritual."

These confessions dwell among us, they are held in the dark spaces between bodies and thoughts. But in Christianity it is only the divine being that has the capacity to contain this amassing of 'wrongdoings', both in the knowledge of God before and after the event. Knowing that puzzle of all knowing, yet pacing the tortuous cycle of confession on the shoulders of the believer seems utterly cruel, a hideous knowing, reflected by an uncanny human gullibility to repeat these words and be bound by such discourse. Remember Nergal Behemoth's words above. Absorbing the sins of others is a containment: it is a hideous gnosis, a knowing of the misery of others and what to do with it; the absorption of the inauthenticity and weakness of the masses.

What do we commit ourselves to in black metal? The opening and consumption of the confessory void. Funeral Mist knew this much: "By supporting Black Metal you support the glorification of rape, incest, war, murder, genocide, oppression fascism corruption. Think twice before buying this divine piece of art! Is it a purchase of dark indulgence? Pay money for an ep and gain permission to be invocated into a Godly project?"

What a transformation can come over us. In anticipation of the eating of flesh and blood, it has a relationship to the sin eater, the shaman who would consume food from the corpse of the dead to allow it to pass to the after life in a pure state, or else the sins of the deceased could flee and roam the sea through demons. A spiritual fellation and cunnulingus of the acts of the deceased. This, a tradition that needs to be reanimated, has its origins in the Celtic people. Its practice documented in the 1911 Britannnica encylopedia records the phenomenon occurring in 1893 in Market Drayton, in Shropshire. In the 17th century at funerals in New York too, the tradition followed Dutch settlers where the *Doed Koecks* bearing the intitals of the deceased were eaten. In the original tradition, the sin eater having consumed food from the corpse and having been paid was beaten and pelted with objects as he left the burial chamber. Do we not continue this tradition when we throw objects onto the stage of the performer who consumes and amplifies our collective vocal stench that is hurled into the void . . . ?

Black Metal has become the sin eater, the role and function regained from the Christian interruption of confession, but elements of the Christian rite remain in the *homologein*. This is where black metal and other forms of extreme metal are still tied to the abject and engage in transgressive behaviour to be rid of it. The serious repetition in BM, the *glossandon homologein*, repeating the words as a confession "Heavy Metal Discourses are detailed repctitive and apparently serious . . . In extreme metal the abject is repetitively examined, only to be destroyed and suppressed." Where Keith Kahn-Harris writes this he also notes that scene members often practice resistance to indulgence, the scene can be based around ideologies of personal empowerment, independence and self control.

Remarkably, this too is the aim of the Christian confession in part, the regaining of a lost esthetical control over the wayward tendencies of the body.

But Black Metal is the voice of the fragmented and disciplined. Black Metal has diversified and in its third wave rejecting stagnations. Going beyond the continuous repetition of words against Christianity, it grows, dealing with subject matter reflecting more and more of the misery of the human condition in all walks of life; see Abgott's recent foray into mafia politics with Godfather in Black and God Dethroned's WW1 story of Paschendale. Absu has always trodden this path with Proscriptor's interest in the occult and magick, mythology and its history. For Absu there has never been a spleen-venting element to their composition, rather it has had at its core story re-telling and the creation of forbidden songs.

Confession inducing the magical ritual of penance the belief in the incantation of forgiveness in the sacramental liturgy- that words have power over the other- that the divine word has efficacy, so too this exists in the self identification declaration of Manannan in Absu's work. Manannan, like the sin eater is a psychopomp, a guide, carrying the dead away over the sea. Confessions originally was part of the sung liturgy- incantation- in a mixture of hymn and proverb for the cleansing of the soul prior to the receipt of the flesh and blood.

In Black Metal in contrast to the Christian confession and absolution, there is no soul to be atoned no restoration to God needed; instead it is an incantation into the void. The black metal event is a confession without need of absolution, redemption, it is a venting, a bloodletting with no prospect of consuming blood. An Anti Corinthian opportunity avails itself: "Whoever receives eats the bread or drinks of the cup of the Lord in an unworthy manner will be guilty of profaning the body and blood of our Lord" (1 Cor. 11:27). If there is adherence to the magic of the sacrament of penance, then the most black inversion is to perform such a rite of consumption with no confession, or to engage in a confession with no eschatology; no direction. We have the power to engage in a Social spring cleaning, cleaning up the mess of others in its subject matter, dealing with issues that one will touch, and as a result harbouring contempt and disdain for a humankind not willing to be honest about its legacy. A mismundanity, hatred of the ordinary that aims to stop us in our tracks with an assault of blandness to which the only appropriate response is revolutionary Black Metal uprising. Endstille's temporary Mexican singer Legubrum (now replaced by Zingultus), complained to me after a gig that he could not cut his throat and spew blood in his performance, instead he had to make do with red wine and the coil of the microphone to present a hanging crucifix position, because the authorities supporting the tour would not let him. Censorship of the forbidden is alive and well. It was all the more hard on him because he wanted to celebrate the Mexican day of the dead and share his blood with others that is a blood that unites us all, a purity that we cannot escape from – he said. It was a pity because it was part of him, his music, his performance and he could not share this with the crowd who deserved to be part of Endstille's body. A sin eaters act suppressed! The event performed prevented from producing an event! This is the event that is neutralised by the state as unwanted priest, but Black Metal has mastery over the event, and its performed speech act. Remember:

Those of the void will re-enter
Clad in robes imprinted with spells
Regress time – degenerate
Founders of mankind . . .
Regress time - Regress time
Those of the void have re-entered!

We can proclaim an invocation to bring forth something out of nothing, but the aim of Black Confession is to annihilate to make nothing out of something that was once: *Prayers to the feeble God whom you once believed in.* Suffocation's lament pointing to nothing ness the purgatorial misery: "As your entity begins its path, there will be no rebirth of your soul, emptiness that clouds your depression, forced to see the light, knowing Jesus wept, only one thing clinging to your mind, the prayers to the feeble god you once believed in."

We are moving from attesting to something that can no longer be attested to (derrida/blanchot) we are bearing witness to that which cannot be witnessed because the project of black metal is to remove the object to which it attests to and contests.

This is the Black Confession and the absence in black absolution.

Jacques Derrida insists that there is a difference between reporting and confession- that something only becomes a confession when one asks for forgiveness, but this requires either a knowing of the sacrament, a knowing of an end result so that there is no surprise, and confession as a ritual becomes devoid of meaning. The compulsion of confession is in the not knowing- not knowing if there will be a response from the divine, hence also the thrill of apostasy- the denial or the rejection of God. There is no need of this if there is a true void- so there is this distinction between void as a nothingness and a void as an unknowing. The Black Confession holds no thrill, it contains the secrets know by all. The sin eater carries the void of unknowing and the void of nothingness as its food, along with the secrets made public.

The Third wave of Black Metal is able to confess an opening to timelessness or oblivion where an ageless continuum, as Jonathan Selzer described Sunn 0)))'s drone output. The Black confession and Black Metal as a collective sin eater feeds over the corpse of modernity, ingesting its vile obsessions, moralism, materialisms and celebrates this amassing of misery, with no purging, no cleansing and no expulsion of social faecal residue. It is a Return to the void, to Absu, the abyss. Those of the void re-enter, but bring the void with them, an entering into a noplace. The sacrament whittled away where reformations removed the flesh and blood to symbolism and penance to symbolic utterance, the progressive removal of Christ to reveal an empty cross and further to the removal of the cross entirely; the consumption and digestion of god so that nothing remains, but the void that was present in the unpresence of presence at the beginning. The direction of Black metal, in this sense ought to move to ever extending iconoclasm. The sacred place of Black Metal is its nowhere- the Black confessions are a precursor to the invocation of that nowhere. Greg Anderson articulates "I hold music to be a sacred and an opportunity to have that connection with the universe in some way. It's the closest thing I've ever ad to a spiritual experience."

The move from the Scapegoat to Celtic confession through Christian confession to the Sumerian Absu mirrors the evolution of Black Metal. It is a move from the sin consumption and its loss to the stranger-void, from a worshipful liturgy of enslavement to a discourse, through to a return of the sin to Absu, the abyss. The Black Metal event is a stranger returning from the void to collect and consume the misery of mankind. This is black confession and Absu-lution.

PINEAL EYE
Lionel Maunz

(Photographs by Oyku Tekten)

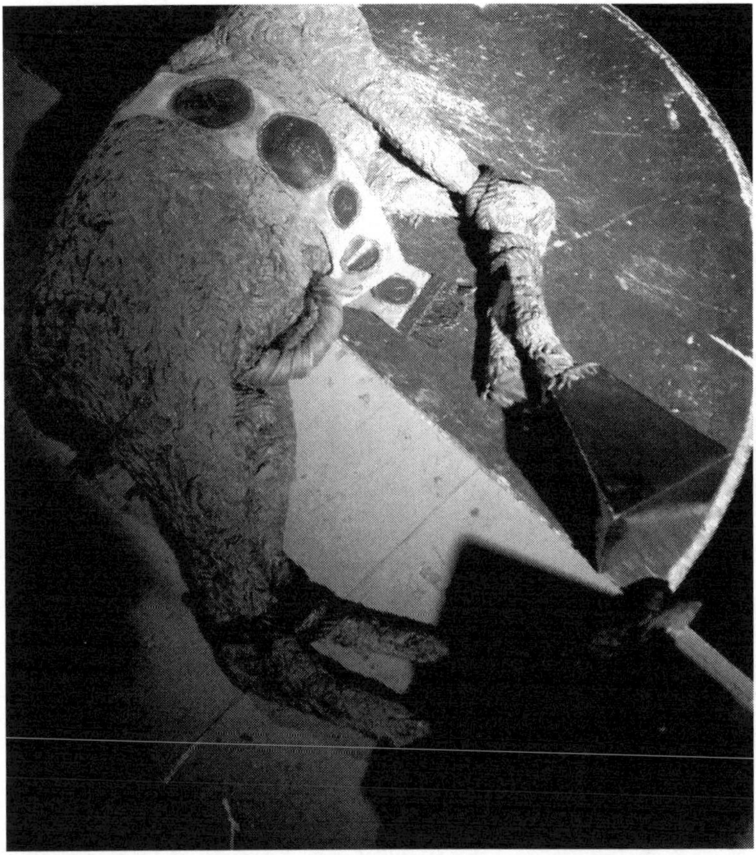

Lionel Maunz – Pineal Eye

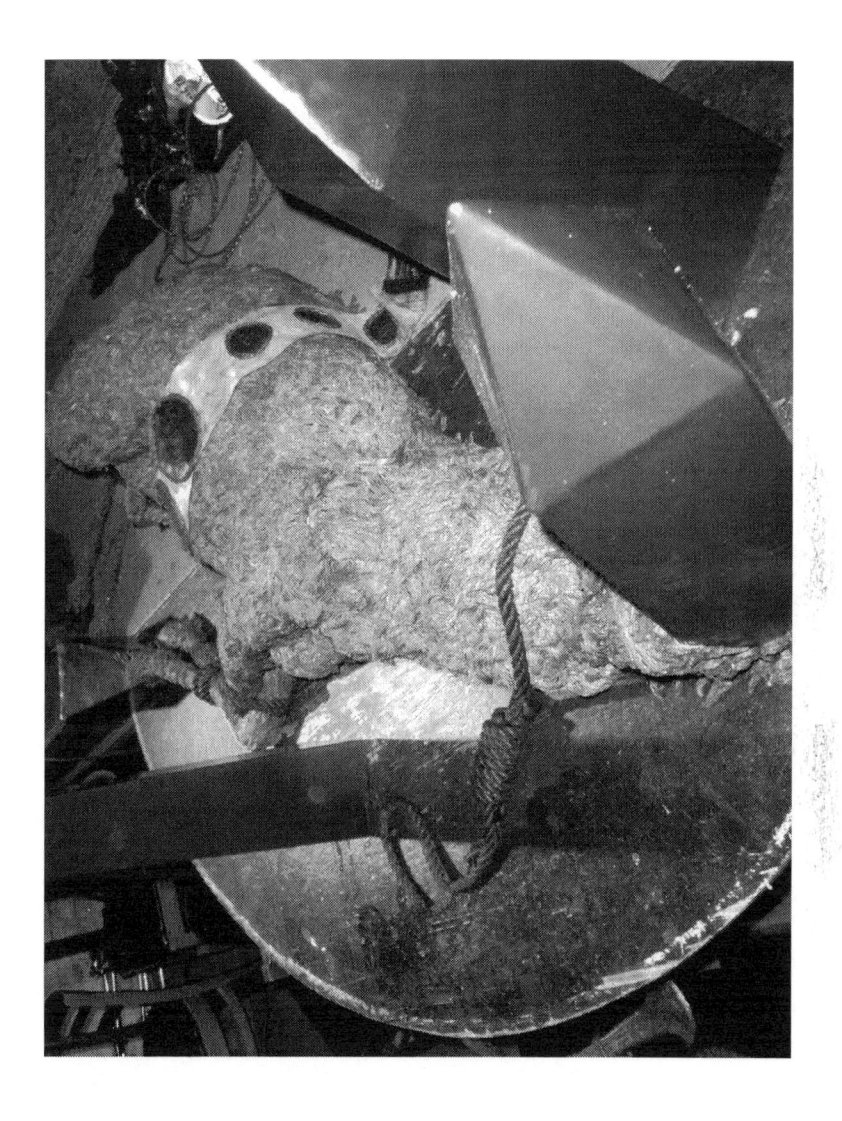

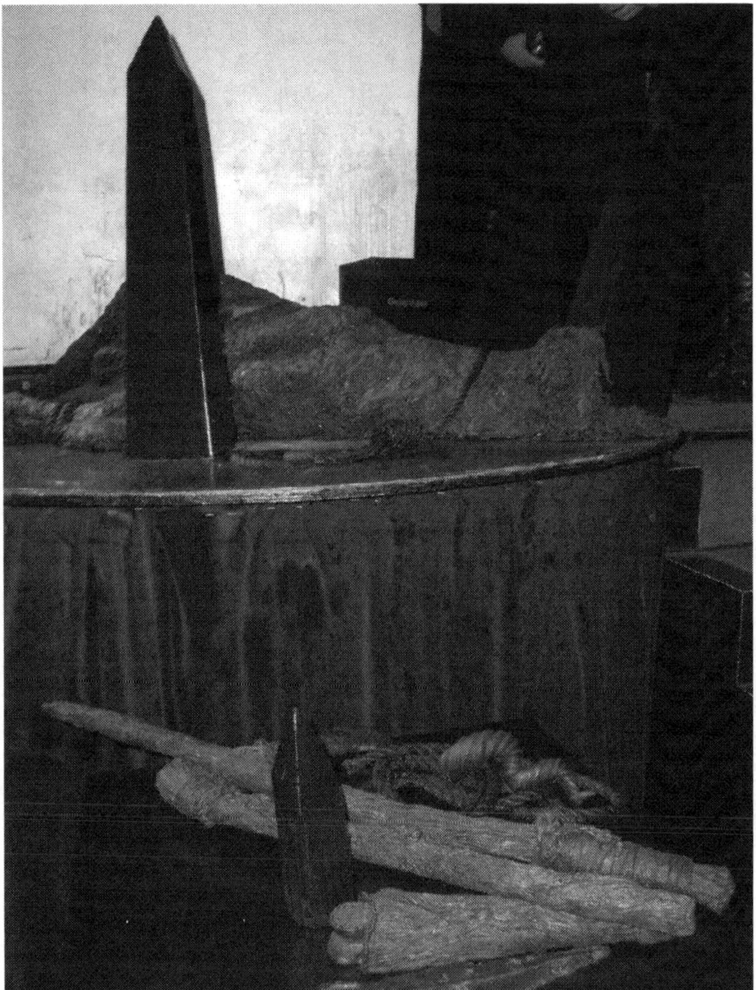

Lionel Maunz – Pineal Eye

SYMPOSIUM PHOTOGRAPHS
Oyku Tekten

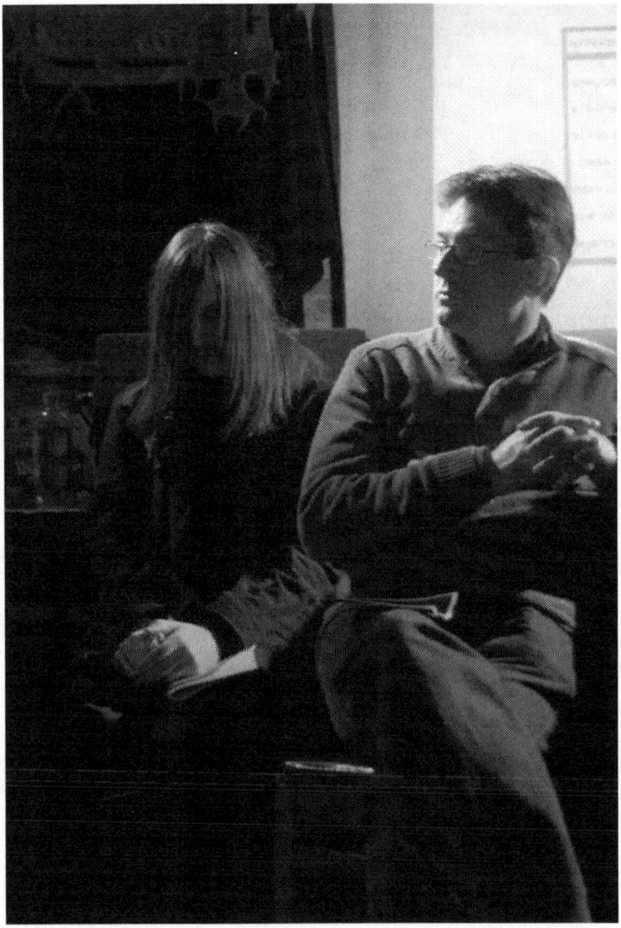

Tekten – Symposium Photographs

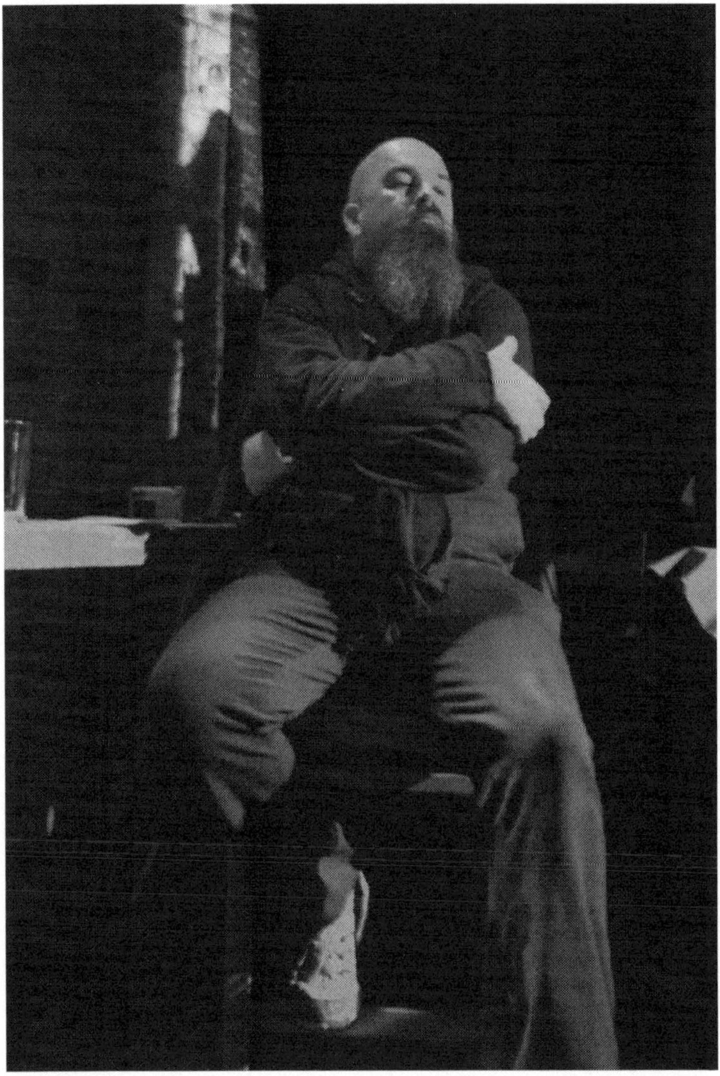

Tekten – Symposium Photographs

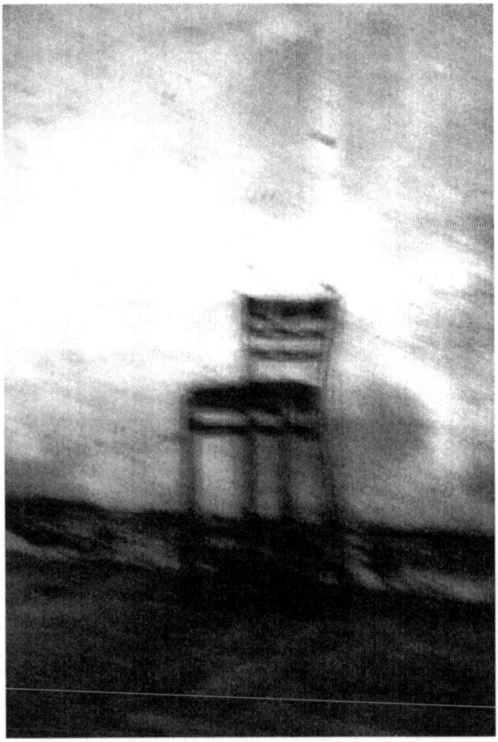

Tekten – Symposium Photographs

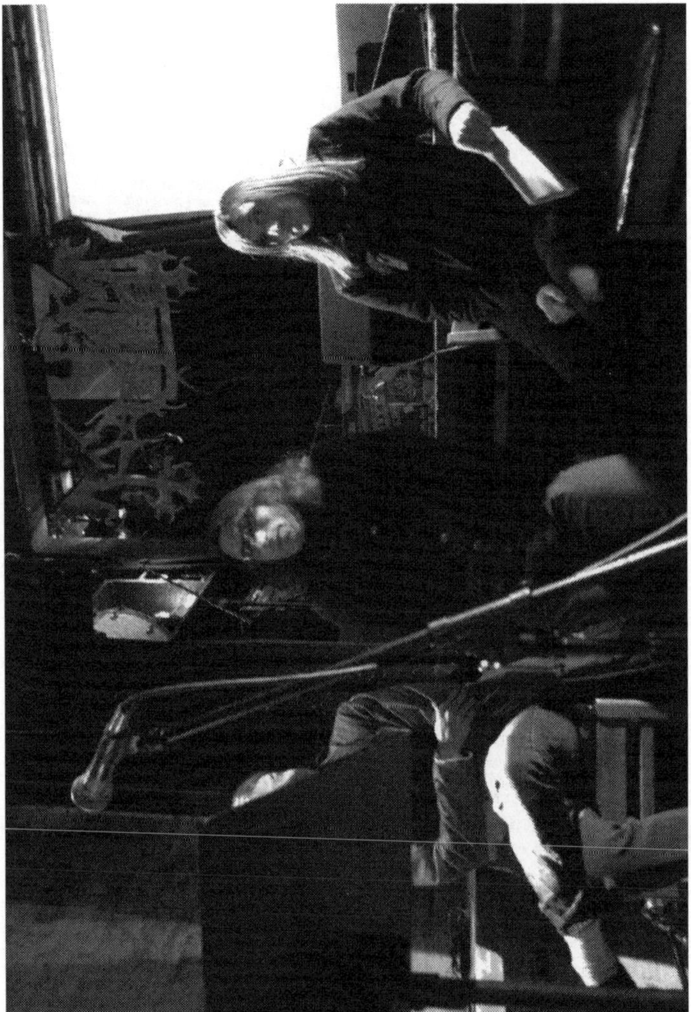

POP JOURNALISM AND THE PASSION FOR IGNORANCE[1]
Scott Wilson

What sucks is when metal is co-opted by wannabe academic nerds

—Chronic Youth[2]

---

[1]Reprinted from *Amusia*, <http://scottwilson-amusia.blogspot.com/2009/08/pop-journalism-and-passion-for.html>

The hostility to academic commentary on popular culture that unites conservatives with pop journalists and bloggers everywhere surfaced again with knee-jerk predictability at the prospect of a Black Metal Theory symposium in Brooklyn this coming December. Both positions assume that either popular culture does not deserve critical inquiry or does not require it. Theory is either redundant or it misses the point which can only be grasped in authentic, inexpressible experience. See also here[3] and here.[4]

All this is jolly good fun and publicity for the event (so thanks again, guys) but I do feel professionally obliged to point out the irony that this hostility is precisely informed by (theoretical) assumptions that are themselves academic, though of a 19th-century Romantic variety. For example, Ben Jonson's trenchant criticisms of his contemporary, Shakespeare, that he a) 'knew small Latin and less Greek' (hence his plays were one big Gothic mess), and b) 'never blotted a line' (and could therefore have done with some serious editing), were taken by the Romantics as evidence of Shakespeare's Natural Genius. True artists must always be essentially unreflecting, intuitive, natural, and art always 'beyond the last instance of criticism' (Frank Kermode). All

---

[2] <http://chronicyouth.com/2009/08/brooklyn-black-metal-symposium-this-december/>
[3] Axl Rosenberg, "Black Metal Gets All Smart N' Shit," <http://www.metalsucks.net/2009/08/19/black-metal-gets-all-smart-n-shit/>
[4] Bram Teitelman, "Black Metal Symposium to Bore Brooklyn To Death," <http://www.metalinsider.net/metalsucksnet/black-metal-symposium-to-bore-brooklyn-to-death>

this does is to empower the Romantic critic who somehow knows (even better than the artist) without having to demonstrate or account for that knowledge, or indeed place it under scrutiny. I assume that this form of criticism is routinely trotted out by pop journo-jocks (often wannabee academic nerds themselves) because it is self-empowering and self-pleasuring. The discourse of the master: 'I want to know nothing about it except that it gives me pleasure'.

Yes indeed it is about enjoyment and authority (and the enjoyment of authority) that is erected on the basis of the bizarre fear that academics might steal it. The fear is strangely paradoxical because, on the one hand, the cloistered 'wannabee nerds' can only press their noses up against the window of authentic experience, and on the other hand, there's the threat that they might 'co-opt' it. The journalist must stick his fingers in his ears and shout it down, or present some caricature. This fear of the academic is completely imaginary and simply (re)produced in order to bolster the journalist's authority and passion for ignorance: passion for the ignorance of the artist, for the incomprehensibility of the work, and the ineffable authenticity of his experience about which she wishes to know nothing except that she experiences it. But that's cool, it's important to be passionate about stuff.

Academics are fans too and can say just as many dumb things as anybody else, not necessarily because they are fans but usually because their discourse has become formulaic and predictable. As such academic discourse can be very boring indeed, especially if you compare it to the popular cultural objects that it talks about (although boredom is often, paradoxically, the interesting marker of a limit). Popular culture, which can also be incredibly boring, is informed (even or especially Black Metal) to varying degrees by academic discourse (art, literature, philosophy, religion etc. etc.), more or less interestingly. Whatever the use artists make of theory, academic discourse can only become interesting if it is modified and changed by its object in some way and is engaged by readers on its own (modified) terms.

This is what we are looking for: Black Metal fucks up academic discourse SHOCK! Now that would be a headline.

SIN EATER, I-V
Karlynn Holland

HIDEOUS GNOSIS

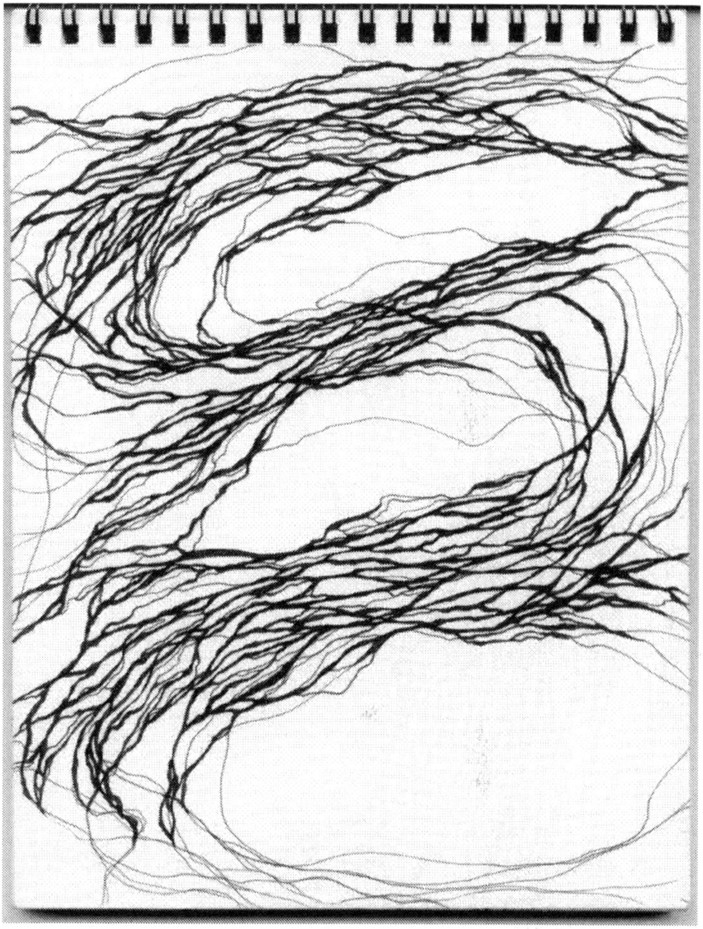

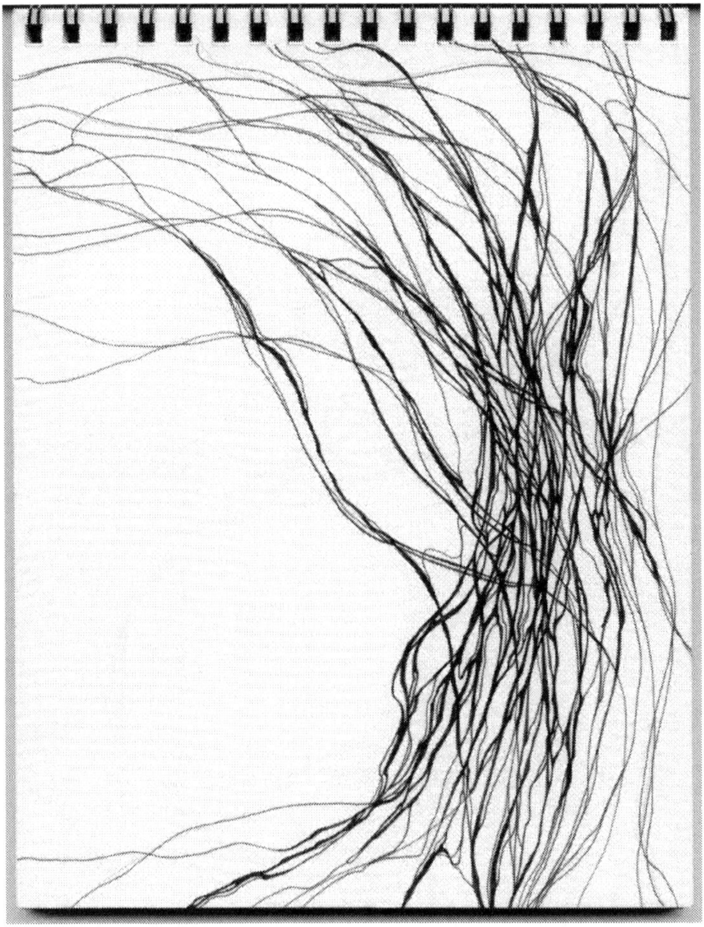

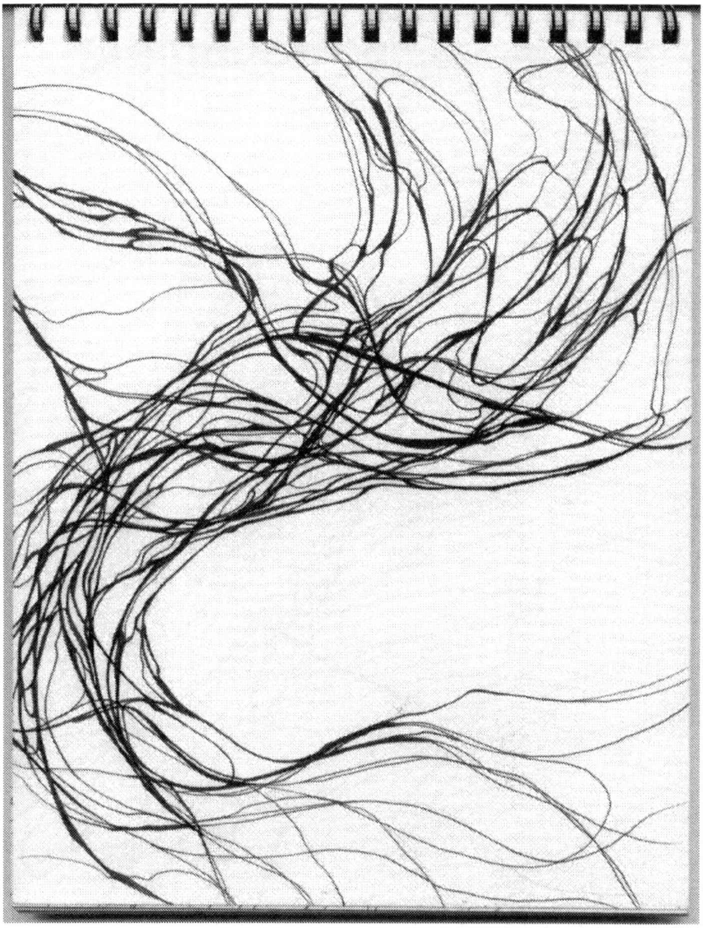

BLACK METAL COMMENTARY
Nicola Masciandaro and Reza Negarestani

(a call for proposals for forthcoming issue of *Glossator*)
http://glossator.org

And thereafter I saw the darkness changing into a watery substance, which was unspeakably tossed about, and gave forth smoke as from fire; and I heard it making an indescribable sound of lamentation.

—*Corpus Hermeticum*

L'OBJET DE L'EXTASE EST L'ABSENCE DE RÉPONSE DU DEHORS. L'INEXPLICABLE PRÉSENCE DE L'HOMME EST LA RÉPONSE QUE LA VOLONTÉ SE DONNE, SUSPENDUE SUR LE VIDE D'UNE ININTELLIGIBLE NUIT. [THE OBJECT OF ECSTASY IS THE ABSENCE OF RESPONSE FROM THE OUTSIDE. THE INEXPLICABLE PRESENCE OF MAN IS THE RESPONSE THAT THE WILL GIVES ITSELF, SUSPENDED OVER THE VOID OF AN UNINTELLIGIBLE NIGHT].

—George Bataille

The burning corpse of god shall keep us warm in the
    doom of howling winds
For we are a race from beyond the wanderers of night.

—Xasthur

CONCEPTS

Vacuum/Void/Abyss: Black Metal and commentary share concern with explicitly spatial forms of emptiness and absence, and with the horror/joy/creativity of being before them. Hans Ulrich Gumbrecht finds a relation to emptiness as the context for commentary's imminent return: "The vision of the empty chip constitutes a threat, a veritable *horror vacui* not only for the electronic media industry but also, I suppose, for our intellectual and cultural self-appreciation. It might promote, once again, a reappreciation of the principle and substance of *copia*. And it might bring about a situation in which we will no longer be embarrassed to admit that filling up margins is what commentaries mostly do—and what they do best" (*The Powers of Philology*). Black Metal similarly fills voids, sounds abysses with its sonic/verbal/visual representations of them. So they share a deeper function beyond explanation/representation, namely, to multiply explanation and representation fractally, to generate more and more perceptual enclosures, spaces within which the unexplainable/unrepresentable is brought into presence.

Liminality/Marginality: Black Metal and commentary situate themselves, and derive power by operating from, margins of genre, history, ideology, knowledge. Both enjoy "unofficial" cultural status. Both destabilize, by holding intimate relation to, categories of the center: truth, onto-theology, "God." Both enjoy forms of authority that are fundamentally ambivalent, safe from attack in a space of irrelevance, yet therefore capable of perfect incursions, the most dangerous unrecognizable raids.

Avant-Garde: The expansion of the margin and the perforation of the boundary associated with Black Metal and commentary provide both with a vanguard front capable of exposing the established order to the corrosive influence of the outside and affecting any outside-oriented determination with the non-escapist influence of the established. To put it differently, since the zone of operation for both Black Metal and commentary is the margin, by expanding the margin of the established order they increasingly expose it to the influence of the beyond. Yet since they also perforate the boundaries, they establish an affect between the beyond and the center. The vanguard in Black Metal and commentary does not merely set itself against the *status quo* in order to make difference (the hallmark of modernism) but rather operates as a form of resistance which is bent on conjuring the potentialities of what has already been grounded and bringing about the obstructed possibilities of beyond *within* the established (primary text, world, idea, etc.). The modernist determination against the *status quo* presumes an emancipatory sublime which adheres to the modernist temporality of progress and the possibility of unilateral determination against the established. For Black Metal, however, this unilateral determination as the vector of modernism is too reliant on the initial possibility of a unilateral separation from the established gravity and the promise of an escape or access to the outside free from the influence of what is already there. Breaking from such promises, Black Metal resorts to action whose scene is here, within and in relation to what is already there, its initiation is not dependent on a hypothetical opportunity, its resources are limited to what is available and its line of determination deflects inward in the direction of what is already there. Black Metal, in this sense, confounds the distinction between expression and praxis. For Black Metal as well as commentary, the deferral of aesthetic or ideological resolution is not compatible with the concrete and conciliatory model of the sublime developed by despotic, fascist and racist movements. Since a notion of the sublime that belongs to another time and is dependent on a promised opportunity or the fulfillment of an initial possibility is prone to ethico-political manipulations, both genres grasp the avant-garde through reworking of the sublime as "beyond within" (Lyotard, *Lessons on the Analytic of the Sublime*).

Arcana/Enclosure: The nexus of erudition and the esoteric. Commentary and Black Metal collude in perverse attachment to sedimentary, occult lore, to what is buried in books, and more generally in relations to lore *as buried*, in need of excavation. This shared loric perversity may be understood on the analogy of archaeology, as a discipline which unearths so as to reinter in the tombs and vaults of its own expertise, which understands by entombing itself in a relation to the object as artifact. So, like the alchemical manuscript, itself often the story of another found-and-lost text, commentary makes itself available via indirection, not generally but for those who want to know, who love to follow the multiplying referential labyrinths of knowing. Similarly, Black Metal delves into obscure discourses only to sing them through the dark veils of its own *trobar clos*, so as to produce and enjoy itself as a hidden relation to the hidden. Hermetic, subterranean, semi-anonymous, Black Metal and commentary pursue parallel adventures in conspiratorial and melancholic epistemic conditions, in erotic relation to their objects as always already lost. At the same time, commentary and black metal, by pro-ducing their arcane or enclosed condition, by bringing it into presence as art, also keep open and play in freedom from it, as modeled in Robert Burton's melancholic and melancholy-curing commentarial *Anatomy*—"I write of melancholy, by being busy to avoid melancholy"—and in the black bile-sweetening music—"a certain melancholy disposition . . . made sweet for us by frequent use of the lyre" (*Letters*)—of the saturnine occultist commentator Marsilio Ficino, who understood "that the melancholy man was uniquely suited to perform the talismanic incantations which he believed were capable of liberating the spirit from the world of appearances" (Robin Headlam Wells, "John Dowland and Elizabethan Melancholy"). Haunted by the principle of *ignotum per ignotius* as its own logical spectre, the clarifying-by-complicating and explicating-by-obfuscating movement of commentary, which is captured in Montaigne's complaint that "everything *swarms* [*fourmille*] with commentaries," is analogous to Black Metal as a motion/anti-motion of artistic expression that articulates from and through enclosure, or, as Dante knew, bubbles to the surface from black depths: "Fixed in the slime they say: 'We were sullen in the sweet air gladdened by the sun, bearing within us the sluggish fumes [*accidioso fummo*]; now we are sullen in the black mire.' This hymn they gurgle in their throats [*si gorgoglian*] ne la strozza, for they cannot speak it in full words" (*Inferno* 7.121-6).

Necrology: Black Metal is usually characterized among its followers and opponents by its ambivalent relationship with death and decay to such an extent that it is often said that the only protagonists in Black Metal are festering corpses. It is the ambivalent relationship of Black Metal with death that gives rise to the most criticized aspect of Black Metal, namely, necromanticism. As a part of vitalistic investment in death, necromanticism involves a liberalist or hedonistic openness toward death in the form of a simultaneously economical and libidinal synthesis between desire and death. Capable of safe guarding the innermost political, economical and libidinal recesses of vitalism, necromanticism simultaneously enchants the necrotic Other with the charm of animation and romanticizes a vitalistic escape through death. Yet Black Metal can also be approached from a more twisted and colder intimacy with death, an impersonal realm where the already-dead finds its voice in the living. The voice of the living, in this case, bespeaks of dejection from a world for which vitalistic ideas are spurious, yet they cannot be simply disillusioned or disenchanted by recourse to death in the form of utter annihilation or solution as termination. Black Metal, in its lyrics, sounds and performances, simultaneously presents the impossibility of this recourse and vitalism's precarious position through the concept of blackening or decay. Aside from Black Metal's necromanticism which usually takes on a medieval gloss, Black Metal's ambivalent relationship with death and decay corresponds with medieval necrology which appears in commentaries of scholastic theology and natural philosophy. More than just assuming a successive role for the medieval commentaries on death, decomposition and macabre, Black Metal can also be examined as a unique genre capable of disinterring the necrological dimensions of commentary. It is in commentary that the dead is impersonally animated according to its own laws and not by the laws of the living. Both Black Metal and commentary genre internalize the concept of decomposition and infinite decay by putting to the test the tolerance or the limit of the world, a text or an idea without completely erasing or silencing it. Here, commentary and Black Metal respectively correspond with an interminable—therefore a limit process—explication or disintegration of a primary source. Such a limit process constitutes the basic principle of decay in which the object degenerates to no end without returning to its constitutive elements (a better and older world), or without becoming silent and ceasing to exist.

Problematicity: Rather than seeking resolving solutions, both Black Metal and the commentary genre operate as functions of the problem. Their approach to their objects, themes, ideas and genres is characterized by relentless problematization. They do not resolve the problematic situations but rather contribute to the internal tension of the problem. Quite literally, they situate themselves as problematical entities. The internal duplicities of Black Metal toward death, (anti-)humanism and extremities are the consequence of such problematical nature which requires means of investigation and commentary other than pejorative, purifying and absolving. Where other musical genres are constantly tempted towards justification and purification (musical, philosophical, aesthetical, etc.), Black Metal tends to bask in *the speculative glory of the problematic.*

Praxis: Whatever their utility, commentary and Black Metal intersect in an essential anti-instrumentality. Commentary and Black Metal make useful, enjoyable products, but their production of them is determined by various kinds of counterimpulses that would unmake production as such, that would perform it freely, at once for itself and for nothing. For commentary, anti-instrumentality shows up primarily in the way it is pursued as praxis, as a way of being with a text that only produces the commentary as a record or residue of an essentially relational "extra-textual" experience, like the reader's marginalia, so often *not* written to be read. But this negative production, production as residue or waste, is exactly commentary's fertility. Formed of the accumulated impressions of innumerable actions and reactions to the text, commentary *accomplishes* nothing and so becomes *capable* of everything. As waves are to the stones that caused them, the gloss is to what it glosses, spreading out in unending uniqueness from the page's unmarkable center, giving witness to depths the undisturbed, undefaced surface cannot. Commentary thus materializes a form of consciousness that may be understood as phenomenological, following Gaston Bachelard's understanding of the *reverberation* of the poetic image as an experience whereby being realizes itself in a movement of reading *becoming* writing: "Through this reverberation, by going *immediately* beyond all psychology or psychoanalysis, we feel a poetic power rising naïvely within us. After the original reverberation, we are able to experience resonances, sentimental repercussions, reminders of our past. But the image has touched the depths before it stirs the surface. And this is also true of a simple experience of reading. The image offered us by reading the poem now becomes really our own. It takes root in us. It has been given us by another, but we begin to have the impression that we could have created it, that we should have created it. It becomes a new being in our language, expressing us by making us what it expresses; in other words, it is at once a becoming of expression, and a becoming of our being. Here expression creates being" (*Poetics of Space*). For Black Metal, anti-instrumentality shows up above all in its paradoxical nihilistic visions of itself, in the identity of being a useless and alienated activity (given the futility of all things and in particular pathetic humanity's imminent demise) that is yet ordered as agency towards the apocalypse and/or universal transformation which renders its own production futile. Whence, for instance, Mortifer's account of Abonus Noctis's latest release as producing in the listener the event it narrates: "*Penumbral Inorgantia* is a chronicling of a man's journey to ancient underground kingdoms haunted by the inhuman entities

that once dwelt therein. He must seek their arcane instruments to rid earth of all organic life after sinking into the abysmal pools of their souls to shed his human frame and assume an elevated, blackened, and immortal state of being, enabling him to eternally reign over the desolation he has created. Each song represents a specific stage in his journey and shall consequently engulf the listener in an experience of metamorphosis into inhumanity"
(http://www.wraithproductions.net/bandpages.htm).

Possession: In Black Metal, all elements from musical to vocal and visual must reflect the voice of the outsider, the indifferent or even the hostile and the incompatible. The explicit distortions and to some extent theatrical discordance of Black Metal are the outcome of the genre's embracing of possession as a conceptual and structural determinant. Referred to by Oesterreich as the "terrible spectacle" (*Possession: Demoniacal and Other*), possession not only suggests the usurpation of one's voice qua possession but also draws a vector of determination that moves from outside to the inside in order to dismantle the self or turn its zone of activity inside-out. It has been objected that since commentary does not necessarily ground a thesis of its own and is basically determined by an external thetic framework (someone else's possession), it is inherently deficient for hosting radical thinking. Yet this is exactly what makes commentary genre a playground for ascesis of thought, for it determines thinking in relation to that which does not belong to the thinker and is indeed exterior to it. In doing so, commentary simultaneously disturbs the hegemonic harmony between reflection and thinking-for-and-by-oneself, and aligns itself with the true contingency of thinking for which the necessity of the thinker does not have an anterior position or a privileged locus.

It is in commentary genre that thinking transmits both voices and contents which are exterior to the thinker yet they do not enjoy a pre-established status either, because commentary entails the concomitant possession of the primary source by an outsider's voice and thereby, creates a speculative opportunity for thinking and writing on behalf of no one. What is usurped in possession is belonging *per se*—as an appurtenant bond between parties—rather than the possession of someone else on behalf of another. Both Black Metal and commentary regard possession as the true vocation of art and thinking.

COMMENTS
<http://blackmetaltheory.blogspot.com/2009/10/hideous-gnosis-schedule-and-flyers.html>

raw, obsolete said...

Hails, Glossator and ShowNoMercyNYC:

It's hard to imagine that Theory can bring much to Black Metal, a fundamentally Romantic and anti-/pre-Theoretic activity. Blackened Theory -- destructive, chaotic evil, inhuman -- is imaginable. Theoried Blackness is harder to imagine. Can the tools of Theory be tools for Blackness?

At least the "symposium" acknowledges an essential truth about Black Metal: it is different than a collection of musical, stylistic, or social tropes.

So the discussions should be rewarding. If only one could cut out the tongues of the West Coast, Experience Music Project-funded types and their friend Sasha Frere Jones before they open their mouths. They believe that they are earnestly trying to understand, not just produce content for capital, but the required understanding is beyond their ken.

November 21, 2009 3:58 PM

Nicola Masciandaro said...

Raw, Obsolete,

Thank you for articulating the precise problem I want the symposium, not to 'address' or 'solve', but to intensify and exacerbate.

As Reza says in the Glosator CFP, . . . to bask in the speculative glory of the problematic.

Nicola

November 22, 2009 10:15 AM

Andreas Bauer said...
I'm amazed, is this supposed to be an academic event?
December 4, 2009 6:20 PM

Nicola Masciandaro said...
Andreas,
Yes and no I suppose. Perhaps para-academic speaking-in-tongues? We will see what happens.
Glad you are amazed.
Nicola
December 5, 2009 6:51 AM

Anonymous said...
fuck, this is hilarious.
In a bad way.
December 7, 2009 3:45 AM

The Return of the Freezing Winds said...
Will there be a table space for merch/distro?
December 7, 2009 3:59 PM

Nicola Masciandaro said...
RFW,
There is no plan for one but you are welcome to set one up.
Nicola
December 7, 2009 4:36 PM

Nicola Masciandaro said...
RFW,
There are some others who want a merch table too. Email me so I can put you in touch.

Blog Comments

Best,
NM
December 7, 2009 6:10 PM

Andreas Bauer said...

While people can and should be meeting to discuss whatever they want, my stomach hurts to think of this as an academic event. 1. what's the reviewing process like? 2. who are your peers? 3. what is their qualification, and - most importantly - 4. why do you think there is sufficient depth in BM to warrant for such a bold title as BM theory? While I agree that BM can be and perhaps should be discussed academically for its contribution to arts & culture, I strongly disagree to claim that BM has any underlying theory, idiologically, politically, spiritually, etc., that you couldn't fit in its entirety on the back of a beer coaster. And although I have been involved in the BM scene for many years myself and listen mostly to BM today, I refuse to recognise any (substantial) intellectual achievements of this movement, because there aren't any - even quoting Nietzsche can't help over this fact.

December 7, 2009 6:50 PM

Nicola Masciandaro said...

Andreas,

Who says this is an academic event? Who says it is not? It is proposed outside of the parameters but with some of the trappings of academia (para-academic and sub/meta-metal perhaps) and for the sake of the "mutual blackening of metal and theory." What this means is for individuals to determine and experience (or not). But it clearly does not mean that theory and metal are to be construed as discrete categories. Instead it insists on some kind of connaturality between the two, a shared capacity for nigredo. Your concern and assumptions about the metal/theory boundary sounds similar to a comment someone made about the symposium at the Full Moon Productions forum: "I thought one puts occult into his black metal, not the other way around." So this says we are doing something *backwards*, but also beautifully suggests (apparently unintentionally) the potentiality of the backwards, in this case the realization of metal as an 'occult'/theoretical tool, which is of course an essential 'fantasy' of metal, especially BM. So the irony here is the possibility of a situation where the 'intellectual' may demonstrate himself to be a more serious and faithful and heavier metalhead (higher atomic number) than the 'fan' who worries anti-intellectually about the former murdering to dissect his god, where the merely cultural metalhead is made anxious by the harmless threat of someone who really believes (and therefore realizes in an essentially a-religious way) what to him is only fantasy or just 'music'. For further thoughts on the metal/theory boundary see the CFP for the forthcoming issue of Glossator on black metal. To answer your points more specifically:

1) There is no review process.
2) People who love and love to think about black metal.
3) A will and capacity for #2
4) Why do you think of reality as so shallow and/or human nature so timid as to be incapable of creating a knowledge- and joy-producing practice called Black Metal Theory? For this there is absolutely no requirement that BM *contain* its own significance as an essence to be simply explicated (BTW, do not hesitate to mail that beer coaster to my campus mailbox) or that BM itself (whatever that is) be the practice of a theory. "Intellectual achievement" ?

Best,
Nicola

p.s. quoting Nietzsche *always* helps: "This -- it turns out -- is *my* way -- where is yours?" -- That is how I answered those who asked me "the way." *The* way after all -- it does not exist!

December 8, 2009 6:56 AM

Anonymous said...

I find this whole thing laughable when you say you agree with "They believe that they are earnestly trying to understand, not just produce content for capital, but the required understanding is beyond their ken." but then put someone as asinine as Liturgy on the event.

Your inability to come together outside of the theoretical trappings of corpses is quite telling. This loose movement doesn't need anymore of your bullshit.

December 8, 2009 9:35 AM

Nicola Masciandaro said...

. . . perpetually exchanging places with Satan, at the mediating position between the possible and the impossible. (link to http://scottwilson-amusia.blogspot.com/2009/12/bpm-4-metaloricum.html)

December 8, 2009 5:46 PM

Anonymous said...

I imagine this to be more an event open to possibilities. Nothing is outside of power's discourses, Black metal signifies as part of the existing order, in the same way as theory. Bringing together both discourses will probably make more sense than most people think.

December 9, 2009 9:23 AM

Anthony Sciscione said...

Well said, latest Anonymous.

All you knee-jerk bitch-and-moaners would do well to form your opinions as to the validity of this convergence after you've come and heard.

Take all, take some and vomit other, take nothing--fine, but wait for the food to be laid out.

December 9, 2009 10:41 AM

Anonymous said...

someone please go along to this with a camera and then post the pics online. I want to see the faces of all the late-onset-puberty dweebs who attend.

December 9, 2009 10:47 AM

Erik Butler said...

In terms of the calendar--and symbolically, too--the event's occurring between the Festival of Lights and pagan Saturnalia. Like Christmas. The revelers have found room at the inn, suckers. Overly earnest academics and sanctimonious metalheads can graze on the nettles outside while we're drinking. Maybe those herd animals, fattened on their own certainty, will wind up on the table. Caveat profanum vulgus.

December 10, 2009 7:58 PM

T. Ulku Tekten said...

I think Black (as a color before anything) contains all the other colors... -It gets dark when you mix them all. And the black can be the absence of colors or the place holder of all colors. It depends how you look at it... if you look at it, of course. Something else can be added to these already defined blackness... or nothing can be added... So what is all the fuss about academic-nonacademic Black Metal? Why is it an unbearable idea of hearing multiple voices on the BM that some of you seem to claim it's your "holy" Black. I do not think the contributers to the conference have the high-pitched voices that command, demand, and, in doing so, territorialize unlike some of "postglossators" here already did.

Someone says BM can't have an underlying theory, ideologically, politically, etc. Yet, this statement itself is reflecting a strong ideological view point since it draws its limits and make its own territory without sparing even a little hole on the wall... And who says that the conference will have an underlying theory? It might and it might not... Neither A nor B. (B as in Black, for non-identification...)

(Let's change the subject!) After writing what I have written, I remembered that I know nothing about BM. But isn't it the point?

Oyku
December 11, 2009 7:31 AM

raw, obsolete said...

In response to Oyku, Black Metal surely _does_ have an ontology. In fact, it is sufficiently powerful that not one of the presenters was able to pull Black Metal outside of its own realm. All they managed to do was to bring theory to Blackness.

It may be that Black Metal is more open to academics and their tools, and the academy is more threatened and blind to Black Metal's power and/over critique. Academics, do you dare to overthrow the Theory that has made you its slaves and hidden from your eyes the glorious horrors of this disgusting world?

December 14, 2009 4:07 AM

Anonymous said...
Haha, this is utter faggotry. You couldn't script it. All of you should drink shit.
December 14, 2009 12:13 PM

Your mother said...
What a bunch of fucking hipster shit! Christ almighty. What is it with assholes having to build altars to every-fucking-thing?
Falsers. All of you.
December 14, 2009 2:42 PM

Anonymous said...
black metal is just a phase for 99% of the people who come to this meeting. to speak of it's origins and history coming from an american elitest (especially new yorker) standpoint is foolhardy at best, black metal was always portrayed as ancient and medieval for a reason, it takes its many roots in the old ways, old religions, and old fags that still talk about the symbolism behind venom doing what they did instead of doing anything themselves, from an occult or really any point of view. to gather and have a little discussion about important albums, feelings, and sentiments and how much it helps you disassociate from your christian culture are all meaningless vices because you subject yourself to them, none of black metal or the values it really pushes are ever forced upon you in this country or in your life unless you will them to. You can argue that BM can and cannot have an underlying theory all you want because in the end, you're critiquing the artist and not the art, and since one man bedroom faggotry is the all important stain on this scene, you'd basically be masturbating in front of the forum you've gathered. pointless and pretentious to no end, but

perhaps if you use this energy towards something positive or meaningful in your life, whether that be to get a job or find a real hobby, i wish you luck, scum of satan's cock.
December 15, 2009 10:16 AM

Anonymous said...
hahaha quoting caina for black metal theory? fuck off falsers
December 15, 2009 10:22 AM

Letter from Andrew White[1]

Socrates: "And is not philosophy the practice of death?"
Cebes: "Certainly"

(from Plato's *Phaedo*)

"Let's annihilate everything, I say. That's my philosophy. God denies the world, and I deny God. Long live nothing, for it is the only thing that exists."

("Nada" from Camus' *State of Siege*)

"It's part of our nature to oppose and not to conform. That's what I consider Satanic, standing for who we are."

(Nergal of Behemoth)

Professor Masciandaro,

Greetings. I am writing in reference to "Hideous Gnosis" – the symposium on black metal. I am a longtime fan of the genre and am currently in prison for murder. My family is Christian and has never approved of my musical tastes. However, my Aunt is a little more liberal and accepting, so as a gift to me, she sent the NY Times article on the symposium titled "Thank You, Professor, That Was Putrid." I was thrilled to death, very excited about an intellectual analysis of black metal – in my opinion, a great idea and very appropriate. As I see it, modern concepts such as existentialism and nihilism, even deconstructionism and postmodernism, tie in very well with extreme metal. Black metal has been an important part of my

---

[1] Ellipses are original. The three citations included here as epigraphs are copied in order from the reverse pages of Andrew's three-page letter.

life. I consider it profound art. For me, it combines nihilistic rage with something resembling beauty and a longing for transcendence . . . Do you enjoy the music? Do you hear what they are trying to do, and at times accomplish? How was the conference? Were many people there? I have to ask if many typical black-clad fans were there? Was there accompanying music playing during down times? I wish I could have been there . . . One thing I think is important to understand about black metal is the arrogance of the fans and those involved. Many are narcissistic. I remember telling my bemused friend how I was one of the dark metal elite. Indeed, there is a song by the band War titled simply "We Are Elite." The whole thing is motivated by a longing to be different, better, special, to transcend the mundane. Such desires often spring from a wounded ego or inferiority issues – a kind of inferiority/superiority complex. People into black metal are often stereotyped as socially inept, unsuccessful with women, picked on, etc. There is a clichéd joke about black metal fans (or even musicians) who live at home with mom (and/or dad). I'm sorry to say I was that guy. Awareness of this just increased the feelings of anger and isolation that led me into the genre in the first place . . . The best analysis I've read previously came from ANUS.com (American Nihilist Underground Society). On the site was a long article titled "The Philosophy of Metal." They also examined the connections between black metal and National Socialism, seeing common roots in romanticism. I have never thought about the connections between black metal and Roman Catholicism, suggested by Professor Erik Butler. I makes sense, though: the ritual, the somberness, the spectacle, the deep connection to the past. It's nothing like the evangelical Christianity I grew up with; I would consider that the "pop" of Christendom. Black metal is like an anti-Roman Catholicism perhaps . . . Again, I appreciate the effort to find the intellectual strains that underlie black metal. The article quotes Italian musician Ovskum as saying, "My music does not come from a philosophy but from a precritical compulsion." I understand where he's coming from; perhaps all art can be seen to come from that place. Nevertheless, I do not believe that is the whole story – the pursuit of the philosophical roots is a worthy one. When speaking of black metal and philosophy, you cannot avoid Nietzsche's influence. Gorgoroth, for instance, takes several song and album titles from his works. There is also an esoteric or mystical strain in black metal; I believe you touched on this in your lecture. Paganism plays a big part in the lyrics and imagery. Broadly speaking, there is in black metal an obsession with the past. I think this can be seen as a reaction against the emptiness and isolation of modern life, not to mention against the weakness of the "herd" whom Nietzsche despised so much. Themes of battle and heroism are common . . . I was interested in the more positive spin on the genre taken by American artists such as Liturgy. The article describes it as moving toward something more "Whitman-esque." Hunter from Liturgy is quoted as speaking of "life and hypertrophy" over "death and atrophy." "Our affirmation is our refusal to deny," he stated. I can appreciate where he's coming from. Personally I have grown from anti-christian rage and despair (feelings which characterized me when I was heavily into the genre and which contributed to the events leading to my incarceration) to a more open, positive view of life. I'm reminded of the more positive side of Camus' thought, namely his idea of revolt. That being said, I have a hard time agreeing with Mr. Hendrix. Black metal is not about the "joyful experience of the continuity of existence." The music can evoke something of a soaring feeling, or even a sense of tranquility amidst the chaos (what my friend called "dark serenity"). The darkness in the music does not have to consume the listener, but it is dark – bleak, angry, violent. This new form of black metal he proposes sounds like something different altogether . . . The article concludes by discussing Mr. Scott's lecture about black metal as part of the ritual of confession. "The black metal event is a confession without need of redemption." "Black metal has become the sin eater; it is engaged in transgressive behavior to be rid of it." Wow! I am still wrapping my mind around that. The "black metal event" has been an important part of my life, for better or worse. I'm glad somebody understands its significance.

Sincerely,

Andrew White

"Black metal ist Krieg" – Nargaroth

Murder Devour I
E.S.S.E.
(Eternal Secret Society of Entities)

Printed in Great Britain
by Amazon